HOTELS OF CHARACTER
AND CHARM IN SPAIN

While every care has been taked to ensure the accuracy of the information in this guide, time brings change, and consequently the publisher cannot accept responsibility for errors that may occur. Prudent travelers will therefore want to call ahead to verify prices and other "perishable" information.

Published in the United States by Fodor's Travel Publications, Inc.
Published in France by Payot/Rivages

Fodor's is a registered trademark of Fodor's Travel Publications, Inc.

ISBN 0-679-03314-9
First Edition

Hotels of Character and Charm in Spain

Translators: Marie Elise Palmier Chatelaine, Anne Norris, Edmund Swinglehurst, Christina Thistlethwayte
Rewriting: Marie Gastaut
Cover design: Fabrizio La Rocca
Front cover photograph: Casa de Carmona, Carmona (Andalusia);
back cover: Hotel Cortijo Aguila Real (Andalusia)

Special Sales

Printed in Italy by Litho Service
10 9 8 7 6 5 4 3 2 1

Fodor's RIVAGES

HOTELS
of Character
and Charm
IN SPAIN

Conceived by
Michelle Gastaut and Fabrice Camoin

Project editor
Michelle Gastaut

Fodor's Travel Publications, Inc.
New York • Toronto • London • Sydney • Auckland

This new 1996 edition details 193 hotels, and the inns and hotels selected are in different categories ranging from simple comfort to 'grande luxe'. We have insisted that our readers can always easily identify the category of each inn or hotel, independently even of its star rating.

You should also note that the prices quoted are those in force at end–1995 and naturally some of them may since have changed. The paradors notably, adjust their prices in the month of March.

As a result all prices quoted should be treated as indicative and when making your reservation by phone or fax, you should ask for the latest detailed rates–also because most hotels quote rates to us **without including VAT (value-added tax), which is 7% or 15% depending on hotel category.** You should also understand that rates quoted for half board and full board are often to be added to the room rates given.

In this new edition we have also given a selection of restaurants and cafés grouped by the major tourist areas, as a complement to your travels and to better appreciate the life of the country. The range of prices given is for a full meal, but excludes drinks.

How to use this guide
We have classified hotels by regions in alphabetical order, and within each region by town or locality in alphabetical order. The number of the hotel page corresponds to the hotel number used on the regional maps, in the Contents pages and in the index of hotel names.

Practical information

All such information (airports, phone & fax numbering system, and exchange rates) is given on page 20.

Please let us know...

If you are attracted by an inn or small hotel not listed in our 1996 guide, and you think it worthy of selection, please tell us about it so that the author may visit it. In like manner, if you are disappointed by any of our selection, please also let us know about it.

EDITIONS RIVAGES
Michelle Gastaut
10, rue Fortia
13001 Marseilles
France

CONTENTS LIST

Contents
Restaurants listing by region
Essential Information
Calendar of Festivals, "Corridas" and Fairs
Map of Spain
Road Maps

Hotels:

CONTENTS

A N D A L O U S I A

A R A G O N

ASTURIAS - CANTABRIA

BALEARIC ISLANDS

CASTILLA MANCHA

CATALUNYA

* Prices shown in brackets are prices for a double room, sometimes with half board or full board. For precise details, go to the page mentioned.

RESTAURANTS

ESSENTIAL INFORMATION

TIME DIFFERENCES

Spain: 6 hours after EST; 1 hours after GMT

TELEPHONE/FAX

To contact your correspondent in Spain from USA:
International 00-34 - Town code ★ - Number wanted (★ but omitting the first number between brackets, used only in internal communications).

LODGING

Paradores: You can contact the central reservation office in Madrid Tel. (9)1-435 9700; fax (9)1-435 9944.

GETTING AROUND BY PLANE

Iberia: Spain's major national airline, flied out of hubs Madrid and Barcelona on both international and domestic routes. In Madrid Tel. (9)1-587 81 56. In Barcelona Tel. (9)3-412 56 67. Aviaco, a subsidiary of Iberia, covers only domestic routes.

WEIGHTS AND MESURES

1 meter (m) = 1.09 yards	1 yards = 0.92 m
1 kilometer (km) = 0.62 mile	1 mile = 1.61km
1 gram (g) = 0.04 ounce	1 ounce = 25g
1 liter = 1.6 quarts	1 quart = 0.94 liter

EXCHANGE

US $1 = 126.58 pesetas (Pts)   100 Pts = $0.80

CALENDAR OF FESTIVALS, 'CORRIDAS' AND FAIRS ★

February
– Cadiz, Sitgès (Barcelona) Carnival.

March
– 'Fallas' Festival of bonfires at Valencia
– 'Semana Santa' (Holy Week). The best-known are those of Seville, Valladolid, Toledo, Murcia, Lorca and Cuenca

April
– Seville fair

May
– Horse Fair at Jerez de la Frontera
– Festival of 'Córdoban patios' at Córdoba
– Fair of San Isidro at Madrid
– 'Romerio de Rocio' (Gipsy festival) at Huelva (no 'Corrida')

June
– Corpus Christi (Catholic festival celebrated throughout Spain). The best-known are those of Granada, Toledo, Málaga – and others.
– 'Hogueras' of San Juan, Burgos fair
– Granada: International Festival of Music and Dance (Alhambra)

July
– Pamplona fair ('Encierro' (Bull-running) and 'Corrida')
– San Jaíme fair at Valencia (Second week of July)
– Villajoyosa: Battle of the Moors and Christians

August
– Málaga fair (end-July, early-August)
– Burgos fair
– Flamenco festival at Jerez de la Frontera

September
– Jerez de la Frontera: Grapes Harvest Festival
– 'Corridas' of Valencia
– Salamanca fair
– Grape harvest fair of Logroño
– 'Corridas' of Barcelona

October

– Fair of the feast of the 'Virgen del Pilar', closing the 'Corridas' season

* This list naturally cannot be exhaustive and only mentions the major events in Spain. Verify dates with the Spanish tourism office, which can also give you a copy of its complete listing of hundreds of local events.

Blay - Foldex
or traveling in France and around the world

15 detailed **regional maps** with index

The easy-to-read **«60kms around»** series

Atlas of France with alphabetical listing of towns

More than 130 **city maps**

maps-plans-guides
40-48, rue des Meuniers
F - 93108 MONTREUIL cedex (FRANCE)
Tél. : (1) 49 88 92 10 - Fax : (1) 49 88 92 09

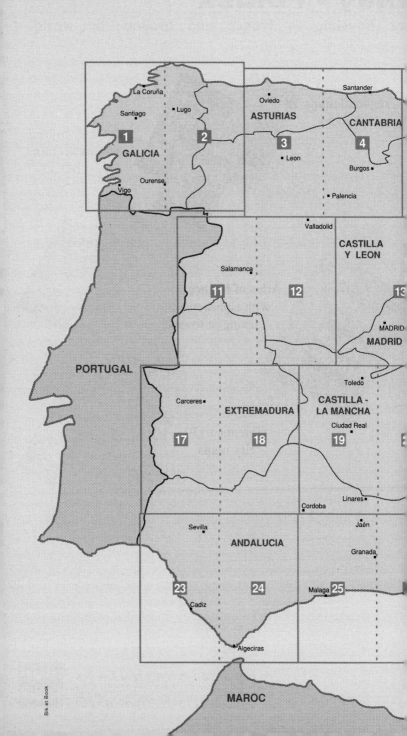

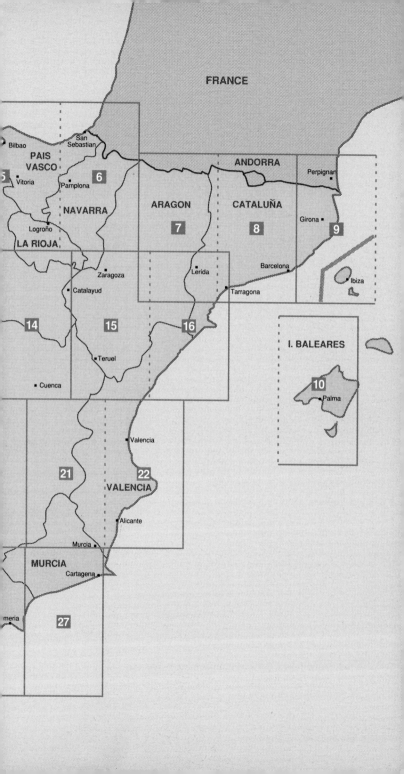

KEY TO THE MAPS

Scale: 1:1,000,000
Maps 30 & 31: scale: 1:1,180,000

MOTORWAYS

❶ Interchange
❷ Half-interchange
❸ Toll-barrier

Kilometre-distance
❶ in total
❷ partial

Motorway
❶ under construction
❷ projected

ROAD CLASSIFICATION

Dual-carriageways

High traffic road

Trunk road

Other road

Road ❶ under construction
     ❷ projected

TOWNS CLASSIFICATION

❶ by the population

— less than 10.000 inhabitants   ○
— from 10.000 to 30.000   ○
— from 30.000 to 50.000   ⊙
— from 50.000 to 100.000   ◉
— more than 100.000   ●
— towns with over 50.000 inh.   ⬠

❷ Administrative

— Chief-town of department   **TARBES**

— Main subdivision of department   **CARPENTRAS**

— Districts   **Combeaufontaine**

— Commune, hamlet   Andrézieux-Bouthéon

ROAD WIDTH

4 carriageways

3 lane or
2 wide lane

2 lane

Narrow road

Kilometre-distance
❶ in total
❷ partial

BOUNDARIES

National boundary
County boundary

TOURISM

Picturesque locality   Chenonceaux

Very picturesque locality   **Amboise**✱

Interesting site or natural curiosity   Roches de Ham

Historic castle

Ruins of outstanding beauty

Abbey

National park

DIVERS

Civil Airport

Dam

Canal

Car-ferries

Motorail

Pass

Summit   ▲ 2392

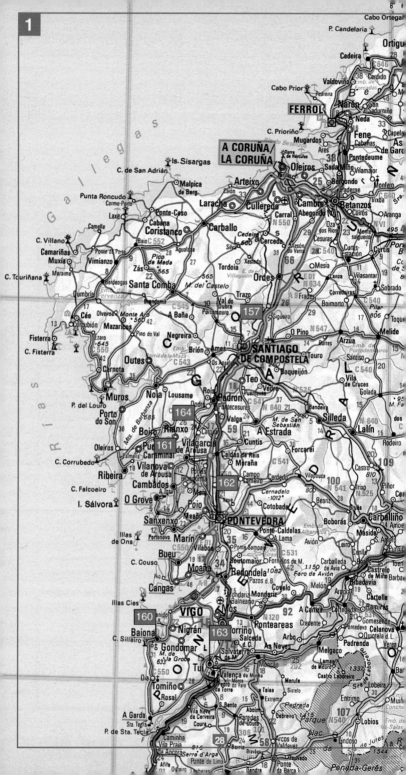

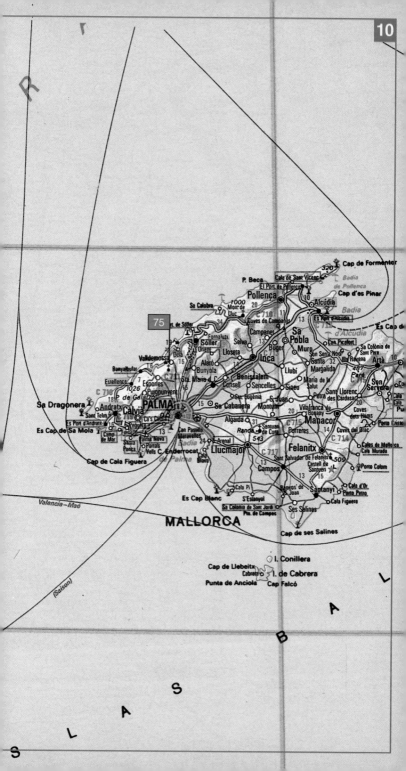

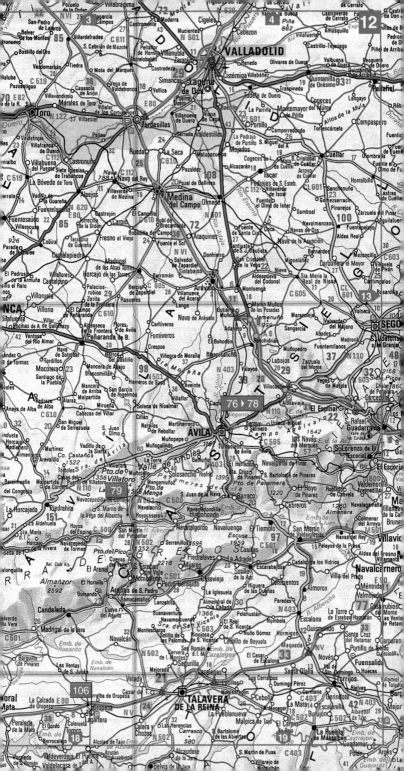

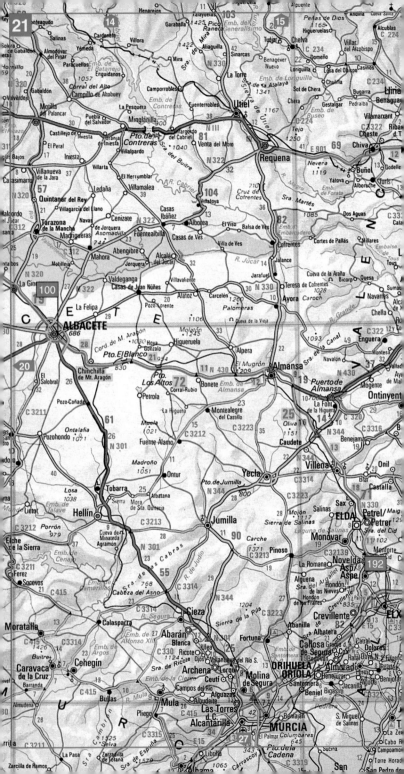

HÔTELS

Hotel Reina Cristina ★★★★

11200 Algeciras (Cádiz)
Paseo de la Conferencia
Tel. (9)56-60 26 22 - Fax (9)56-60 33 23
Sr Fernandez

Rooms 140 with air-conditioning, telephone, bath, WC and TV. **Price** Single 8,000-10,000Pts, double 13,500-17,500Pts, suite 21,000-27,000Pts. **Meals** Breakfast 1,750Pts, served 7:15-10:30; half board + 4,450Pts, full board + 5,700Pts. (per pers.). **Restaurant** Service 13:00-15:30, 20:00-22:00; also à la carte. Specialties: regional and international cooking. **Credit cards** All major. **Pets** Small dogs allowed in the rooms. **Facilities** Swimming pool, tennis, minigolf, sauna, parking. **Nearby** Beaches of Getares, Chaparral, Los Ladrillos, El Rinconcillo - Ceuta - The road from Algeciras to Ronda. **Open** All year.

This hotel is haunted with memories as its history began in 1890 when the government commissioned a British company to build the railway from Bobadilla to Gibraltar. Lodging in Algeciras during the work, the director was so attracted by the region that he decided to build a hotel here. The setting for the Algeciras Conference in 1906 and a haunt of spies during the war, it has now recovered all its peace and quiet. Large gardens planted with pine and cypress trees surround the hotel, which has retained its comfortable, rather British style. Its principal charmes in the fact that it is a haven in an all too touristic region.

How to get there (Map 24): 124km southeast of Cádiz via N430; 200 meters from the port.

Parador Casa del Corregidor ★★★

11630 Arcos de la Frontera (Cádiz)
Plaza de Espana
Tel. (9)56-70 05 00 – Fax (9)56 70 11 16
D. Perez Moneo

Rooms 20 with air-conditioning, telephone, bath, WC, TV and minibar. **Price** Single 8,800Pts, double 13,000-13,500Pts. **Meals** Breakfast 1,200Pts, served 7:15-10:30; half board + 4,300Pts, full board + 6,375Pts. (per pers.). **Restaurant** Service 13:00-15:30, 20:00-22:30; menu 3,200Pts, also à la carte. Specialties: regional cooking. **Credit cards** All major. **Pets** Dogs not allowed. **Facilities** Parking. **Nearby** Church of Santa Maria in Arcos de la Frontera - Jerez de la Frontera - Bornos - Monastery of the Cartuja - Villamartin (wine cellars of Pajarete) - Càdix. **Open** All year.

Arcos de la Frontera is on the summit of a granite promontory surrounded by the Guadalete River, in the midst of a Mediterranean landscape of vines, orange and olive trees. The hotel is in town but thanks to its location on the edge of a cliff, it forms a natural balcony with a superb view. It is a very old building but has been sumptuously reconstructed while retaining its original architecture. The panorama can be enjoyed from the lounges, bar, dining room, and the best rooms which have terraces. Close to Jerez de la Frontera, this is a good center for visiting the bodegas and sherry wine cellars of the region.

How to get there *(Map 24): 65km northeast of Cádiz via A4, exit Jerez de la Frontera, then N342; opposite the Ayuntamiento (town hall).*

Hotel El Convento ★

11630 Arcos de la Frontera (Cádiz)
Maldonado, 2
Tel. (9)56-70 23 33 – Fax (9)56-70 23 33
Sra Moreno

Rooms 8 with telephone, bath, WC, and TV. **Price** Single 4,500-6,000Pts, double 6,000-7,500Pts. **Meals** Breakfast 300-700Pts, served 8:30-10:30. **Restaurant** Service 13:00-16:00, 19:00-22:00; menu 2,500-3,000Pts, also à la carte. Specialties: Ajo a la comendadora - Sopa de clausura - Pierna de cordero. **Credit cards** All major. **Pets** Dogs not allowed. **Facilities** Parking. **Nearby** Church of Santa Maria in Arcos de la Frontera - Jerez de la Frontera - Bornos - Monastery of the Cartuja - Villamartin (wine cellars of Pajarete) - Càdix. **Open** All year.

The Hotel El Convento occupies part of the convent of Monjas de Clausuras Mercedarias Descalzas, built in the 17th century. A small hotel with only eight bedrooms in a typically Andalusian style, a simple family atmosphere is found here, along with excellent home cooking. In a historically classified village and completely free from cars, it is just a few paces from several listed national historical monuments. The village is full of charm and the hotel is one of those that one dreams of finding on a journey in southern Spain. Seville is just 70km away !

How to get there *(Map 24): 59km northeast of Cádiz via A4, exit Jerez de la Frontera, then N342 to Antequera.*

Los Olivos ★★★

11630 Arcos de la Frontera (Cádiz)
Paseo de Boliches, 30
Tel. (9)56-70 08 11 - Fax (9)56-70 20 18
Sr J. A. Roldan

Rooms 19 with air-conditioning, telephone, bath, WC, TV and minibar. **Price** Single 3,650-4,235Pts, double 6,650-8,470Pts. **Meals** Breakfast 600Pts, served 8:00-11:00. **Restaurant** See p. 194. **Credit cards** Amex, Visa, Eurocard and MasterCard. **Pets** Dogs not allowed. **Facilities** Parking. **Nearby** Church of Santa Maria in Arcos de la Frontera - Jerez de la Frontera - Bornos - Monastery of the Cartuja - Villamartin (wine cellars of Pajarete) - Càdix. **Open** All year.

An astonishing small Andalusian town, Arcos de la Frontera aligns its white houses on the crest of the plateau overlooking the Guadalete River. The town has conserved some beautiful remnants of its Moorish past and its magnificent church in the flamboyant Gothic style (Santa Maria de la Asunción) is well worth a visit. The hotel is simple but all is arranged in good taste: cane furniture in the lounge-gallery that surrounds the interior patio, and rather monastic rooms that very well maintained. Some rooms overlook the river. Prices are reasonable.

How to get there *(Map 24): 65km northeast of Cádiz via A4, exit Jerez de la Frontera, then N342.*

Cortijo Fain ★★★

11630 Arcos de la Frontera (Cádiz)
Caret. Algar, km 3
Tel. (9)56-70 11 67 - Fax (9)56-70 11 67
Sra Gil de Zalba

Rooms 10 with bath and WC. **Price** Double 16,100Pts. **Meals** Breakfast 1,000Pts. **Restaurant** Service 13:00-16:00, 19:00-23:00; menu 4,000Pts, also à la carte. Specialties: regional cookong. **Credit cards** Amex, Visa, Eurocard and MasterCard. **Pets** Dogs allowed. **Facilities** Swimming pool, parking. **Nearby** Church of Santa Maria in Arcos de la Frontera - Jerez de la Frontera - Bornos - Monastery of the Cartuja - Villamartin (wine cellars of Pajarete Càdix). **Open** All year.

This large property situated 3km from Arcos de la Frontera is not a typical hotel, but ten rooms have been opened in this beautiful 17th-century farm for the use of guests, who can also take part in the daily life of the estate. The rooms are very large and each has a lounge and open fireplace, and all are comfortably arranged and decorated in the best Andalusian style. Two have their own private terraces. Guests can also avail of the library, which, with its 10,000 volumes, is one of the finest private collections in Spain. The house, with its white-walled setting covered with bougainvillea, is surrounded by olive trees which make for very pleasant walk's. In summer the swimming pool can also be used while horse riding is available in the Campos Andalus throughout the year.

How to get there *(Map 24): 68km northeast of Cádiz via A4, exit Jerez de la Frontera, then N342 and Algar road for 3km.*

Casa Convento la Almoraima ★★★★

11350 Castellar de la Frontera (Cádiz)
Tel. (9)56-69 30 50 – Fax (9)56-69 32 14
Sr Montoya

Rooms 11 with telephone, bath, and WC. **Price** Single 8,000Pts, double 13,000Pts. **Meals** Breakfast 750Pts, served to 11:00 ; half board + 3,500Pts, full board + 6,500Pts. (per pers.). **Restaurant** Service 13:30-17:00, 17:00-21:00; menu 3,500Pts Specialties: Game. **Credit cards** All major. **Pets** Dogs allowed. **Facilities** Swimming pool, minigolf, hunting, fishing, parking. **Nearby** Medina Sidonia - Benalup de Sidonia - Costa de la Luz from Càdiz to Tarifa - Algeciras - Gibraltar. **Open** All year.

This ancient convent founded in 1603 has had a rather disturbed past. In the 19th century the Spanish government sold all the possessions of the Friars and it became a private estate. In 1972 it became the hunting lodge of a leading Spanish citizen, from whom it was expropriated in 1982. Nevertheless, a very special atmosphere reigns in this house where everything has been maintained in its original state. Very well equiped to receive its guests, it has a swimming pool, tennis court, billiard room, and a music lounge. Horses and a Land Rover are at your disposal to discover the 16,000 hectares (62 square miles) of the largest 'latifundium' (landed property) in Europe, where deer, stags and wild sheep roam in full freedom, while one can also fish and hunt. On your holiday road in Andalusia, this is an ideal staging post to relax for a few days.

How to get there (Map 24): 145km southeast of Cádiz via N340 to Algeciras, then after 12km towards Jimena de la Frontera for 9km; opposite the Factoria de Corcho (cork factory).

Hotel Jerez ★★★★★

11400 Jerez de la Frontera (Cádiz)
Avenida Alcalde Alvaro Domecq, 35
Tel. (9)56-30 06 00 - Fax (9)56-30 50 01

Rooms 121 with air-conditioning, telephone, bath, WC, cable TV, minibar; elevator. **Price** Single 8,000-10,000Pts, double 13,500-17,500Pts, suite 21,000-27,000Pts. **Meals** Breakfast 1,750Pts, served 7:15-10:30; half board + 4,450Pts, full board + 5,700Pts. (per pers.). **Restaurant** Service 13:00-15:30, 20:00-22:00; carte. Specialties: regional and international cooking. **Credit cards** All major. **Pets** Small dogs allowed. **Facilities** Swimming pool, tennis, parking. **Nearby** Real Escuela Andaluza del Arte Ecuestre (Royal Andalusian School of Equestrian Art) de Jerez de la Frontera; Jerez's wine cellars (Bodegas de Xéres de Gonzalez Byass, Pedro Domecq, Williams Humbert); Feria del Caballo (Horse Fair 4/6 May); Flamenco Festival in August; Vintage Festival in September- Càdiz - Arcos de la Frontera - Bornos - La Cartuja - Sanlúcar de Barrameda. **Open** All year.

Only 4km from the town center in a modern building in the residential area, this hotel in the Ciga chain enjoys a wonderfully calm setting. The bedrooms are luxurious and all have a balcony, most of which look onto the garden and its beautiful lawns, palm trees and exuberant plants, all protected from the road by thick hedges. You can also enjoy the large swimming pool at your leisure. The restaurant offers excellent seafood dishes, accompanied by the well known wines of the area, world-renowned cellars. Service and comfort are very high quality, but one should remember that prices/rates are marked up by 30% during the Feria.

How to get there *(Map 24): 35km northeast of Cádiz via A4, exit Jerez de la Frontera; 4km from town center.*

Hotel Serit ★★

11400 Jerez de la Frontera (Cádiz)
Avenida Higueras, 7
Tel. (9)56-34 07 00 – Fax (9)56-34 07 16
Sra Acosta Jimenez

Rooms 35 with air-conditioning, telephone, bath, WC, TV, safe; elevator. **Price** Single 4,500-7,000Pts, double 5,600-10,000Pts. **Meals** Breakfast 400Pts, served 8:00-11:00. **Restaurant** See p. 195. **Credit cards** All major. **Pets** Small dogs allowed. **Facilities** Parking (800Pts). **Nearby** Real Escuela Andaluza del Arte Ecuestre (Royal Andalusian School of Equestrian Art) of Jerez de la Frontera; Jerez's wine cellars (Bodegas de Xéres de Gonzalez Byass, Pedro Domecq, Williams Humbert); Feria del Caballo (Horse Fair 4/6 May); Flamenco Festival in August; Vintage Festival in September - Càdiz - Arcos de la Frontera - Bornos - La Cartuja - Sanlúcar de Barrameda. **Open** All year.

Jerez is a town made famous by the wine carrying its name: 'sherry' (slightly deformed by the British because of its impossible pronunciation). It also boasts a riding school with a great reputation, as well as the attractions of the vine. The annual Feria in honor of the horse is one of the most important in Andalusia. In a small street close to the center, the Serit is one of those hotels with a discreet facade but whose appeal is evident once the front door is opened. The comfort, calm and the reasonable rates all appeal. Although rather standardized, the rooms are agreeable and all have a small antichamber separating them from the bathroom. A corner lounge on the ground floor has comfortable sofas and a marble floor, while beautiful photographs on the walls recall different aspects of Jerez life.

How to get there *(Map 24): 35km northeast of Cádiz via A4, exit Jerez de la Frontera; next door to La Plaza de las Angustias.*

Posada de Palacio ★★★

11540 Sanlúcar de Barrameda (Cádiz)
Calla Caballeros, 11
Tel. (9)56-36 48 40 - Fax (9)56-36 50 60
Sr Navarrete

Rooms 11 with bath and WC. **Price** double 8,500Pts, suite 12,000Pts. **Meals** Breakfast 700Pts, served 8:30-11:30. **Restaurant** See p. 196. **Credit cards** Diners, Visa, Eurocard, MasterCard. **Pets** Small dogs allowed. **Facilities** Swimming pool, tennis, parking. **Nearby** Bodegas (Hijos de A. Pérez, Meijía, Manuel Garcia Monje, Rafael Reig y Cia) in Sanlùcar; Feria of the Manzanilla in May - Jerez de la Frontera - Monastery of Nuesta Señora de Regla close Chipiona - Beaches of Rota - Bornos - La Cartuja - Sanlúcar de Barrameda. **Open** 1. Mar - 6. Jan.

Sanlúcar de Barrameda is an aristocratic town whose reputation is due to its churches and excellent cellars, as well as its very beautiful houses. One of these houses has been converted into a posada with a great deal of love and taste by a very attractive young couple, who have respected the original architecture of the house. You are immediately won over by the patio and one feels comfortable in the welcoming rooms, even though their comfort does vary. The best, strangely, is on the ground floor with a large window onto the street. And as this is a region of cellars, there is a bar of course with a few tables in the white and flowered courtyard.

How to get there *(Map 23): 121km south of Seville via A4, to Jerez de la Frontera, then C440.*

Hotel La Solana

11360 San Roque (Càdiz)
Ctra. Cádiz-Málaga, km 116,450
Tel. (9)56-78 02 36 – Fax (9)56-78 02 36
M. José A. Ceballos

Rooms 13 and 7 suites with bath, TV and minibar. **Price** Single 8,000Pts, double 10,000Pts, suite 12,000Pts. **Meals** Breakfast 600Pts, served 9:00-11:00. **Restaurant** Only for residents. Service 14:00-16:00, 21:00-23:00; menu 2,500Pts. Specialties: Home cooking. **Credit cards** Amex, Visa, Eurocard, MasterCard. **Pets** Small dogs allowed. **Facilities** Mediterranean and Atlantic beaches - Castellar - Sierra of Cádiz - Toros road- Tarifa andt Sotogrande - Alcaidesa and San Roque golf course (18-hole). **Open** All year.

A painter and sculptor of talent, José Cetallos has transformed this beautiful country residence into a hotel, whose 20 hectares of land are situated in the center of the Campo de Gibraltar. One is first attracted by the quality of the decoration, a skilful mix of 'High Period' furniture, magnificent carpets, paintings and bronzes by the master of the house, along with the numerous personal acquisitions that make a fine collection. The interior patio is exquisite with its jacarandas and daturas in superb colors. A little further away is the swimming pool near the cork-oak and eucalyptus trees. Whether on the ground floor, on the patio or on the second floor, all the rooms are attractive. At La Solana there is a particularly calm atmosphere marked by the owner's own personality. In this region of sometimes excessive temperatures and grandiose landscapes (Gibraltar and the African coast), you will feel sheltered here in such a refreshing and cultivated environment.

How to get there (Map 24): 15km from Algeciras towards Málaga-Cádiz. Via N340 exit at km 106.5 to the right; from the other direction, at km 117, take the autoway in the reverse direction and then exit.

Hotel Convento de San Francisco ★★★

11150 Vejer de la Frontera (Cádiz)
La Plazuela, 6
Tel. (9)56-45 10 01/02/03 – Fax (9)56-45 10 04
Sr Garcia Alcedo

Rooms 25 with telephone, bath and WC. **Price** Single 6,000Pts, double 7,650Pts. **Meals** Breakfast 800Pts, served 7:00-11:30; half board + 2,185Pts, full board + 3,950Pts. (per pers.). **Restaurant** Service 13:30-15:30, 20:30-23:00; closed Tues; carte: 3,400-4,200Pts. Specialties: seasonal cooking. **Credit cards** All major. **Pets** Dogs not allowed. **Facilities** parking. **Nearby** Medina Sidonia - Benalup de Sidonia - Costa de la Luz from Càdiz to Tarifa - Càdix; Campo San Andrès golf course (18-hole). **Open** All year.

On a steep hill stands an old 17th-century Franciscan convent now transformed into a hotel. One is first of all impressed by the entrance which happily has conserved its multicolored mosaics. The lounges have kept their grandiose aspect, even if the furniture has. Particular care has however been taken with the vast bedrooms, where simplicity and the rustic have been melded together, notably with the usage of open stonework. The small town of Vejer is classified as a 'historical-artistic monument' and has a rather wild charm with its windmills. To lovers of folklore it offers a full calendar of fêtes and fairs.

How to get there (Map 24): 53km southeast of Cádiz via N430.

A N D A L U C I A

Hotel Alfaros ★★★★

14001 Córdoba
Calle Alfaros, 18
Tel. (9)57-49 19 20 - Fax (9)57-49 22 10
M. David Madrigal

Rooms 133 with air-conditioning, telephone, bath, WC, cable TV, safe and minibar; Handicap access; elevator. **Price** Single 9,200-11.800Pts, double 11,500-14,800Pts. **Meals** Breakfast 1,100Pts, served 9:00-11:00. **Restaurant** Service 13:30-15:30, 20:30-23:00; menu 1,920-2,650Pts, also à la carte. **Credit cards** All major. **Pets** Dogs not allowed. **Facilities** Swimming pool, garage, parking. **Nearby** Córdoba: Fiesta de los Patios (5-15 May); Feria de Nuestra Señora de Fuensanta (Sept.) - Medina Azahara(6km) - Monastery of San Jerónimo - Las Ermitas de Córdoba (13km) - Sanctuary of Santo Domingo de Scala Dei - Los Villares golf course (18-hole). **Open** All year.

One can only know Spain and Andalusia well by visiting Córdoba, the former capital of the Moslems whose cultural and spiritual empire stretched from Rome to Africa, and further to the west. The mosque–cathedral is alone worth the journey but the town with its flowered patios, wrought ironwork and 'azuleros' also has a lot of charm. The Alfaros Hotel has sought to transpose all such influences into a modern decor, which has created a luxurious and theatrical hotel. Great comfort reigns throughout the hotel which also offers all the latest technology: fax connection, TV satellite dish and magnetic card access to rooms, etc.. All rooms are spacious and light. The swimming pool is worthy of an Arabian Gulf palace. Along with the full-time service, this is a great hotel.

How to get there *(Map 19): in the center of town.*

Hotel Conquistador ★★★★

14003 Córdoba
Calle Magistral González Frances, 15/17
Tel. (9)57-48 11 02 - Fax (9)57-47 46 77
Sr P. Albujer

Rooms 103 with air-conditioning, telephone, bath, WC, TV and minibar. **Price** Single 9,000-11,000Pts, double 12,500-15,500Pts, suite 18,000-22,000Pts. **Meals** Breakfast 1,000Pts, served 7:00-11:00. **Restaurant** See p. 194. **Credit cards** All major. **Pets** Dogs not allowed. **Facilities** Parking (900Pts), sauna (1.000Pts). **Nearby** Córdoba: Fiesta de los Patios (5-15 May); Feria de Nuestra Señora de Fuensanta (Sept.) - Medina Azahara(6km) - Monastery of San Jerónimo - Las Ermitas de Córdoba (13km) - Sanctuary of Santo Domingo de Scala Dei - Los Villares golf course (18-hole). **Open** All year.

This is the former Hotel Adarve which the new owners have baptized as the Conquistador. All the amenities however remain the same while the prices, in contrast, have been lowered a little. Adjoining the mosque, this modern hotel was nevertheless built in an Andalusian Moorish style using both mosaics and marquetry to a very successful effect. All the reception rooms give onto a charming patio where there are columns, a fountain and luxurious vegetation. The rooms are designed with elegance and some, such as Numbers 110, 210 and 310, are very luxurious with marble bathrooms, and a view onto the patio. Those on the facade have a view of the mosque that is illuminated at night-time.

How to get there (Map 19): in the old town.

A N D A L U C I A

Hotel Amistàd Córdoba ★★★★

14004 Córdoba
Plaza de Maimònides, 3
Tel. (9)57-42 03 35 - Fax (9)57-42 03 65
Sr. Billagran

Rooms 69 with air-conditioning, telephone, bath, WC, TV and minibar; elevator. **Price** Single 12,000Pts, double 15,000Pts. **Meals** Breakfast 1,200Pts, served 7:30-11:30. **Restaurant** Service 12:00-16:30, 20:30-23:30; carte. **Credit cards** All major. **Pets** Dogs not allowed. **Facilities** Garage (1,000Pts). **Nearby** Córdoba: Fiesta de los Patios (5-15 May); Feria de Nuestra Señora de Fuensanta (Sept.) - Medina Azahara(6km) - Monastery of San Jerónimo - Las Ermitas de Córdoba (13km) - Sanctuary of Santo Domingo de Scala Dei - Los Villares golf course (18-hole). **Open** All year.

The Amistàd of Córdoba is a very new hotel in the Barrio dela Judería, the former Jewish ghetto with its white and flowery narrow streets, giving on to the famous Córdoban patios. Do not fail to visit the well-known Mezquita (cathedral-mosque) in this quarter, and also the synagogue, one of the most celebrated in Europe along with that of Toledo. The hotel is close by and even if the buildings are 18th century, entry is still made via an arch pierced in the ancient Moorish wall. To shelter the hotel, two former residences have been joined but the interior mudejar patio has been preserved. All amenities are resolutely contemporary but with some references to local style, as with the suite of arcades in the main lounge. The decor is contemporary, elegant and very sober. The rooms are much warmer, spacious and also just as refined. Comfort and personalized services are the main priorities, and this is one of the best hotels in Córdoba.

How to get there (Map 19): *143km Northeast of Sevilla.*

14

A N D A L U C I A

Hotel Gonzalez ★★

14003 Córdoba
Manriquez, 3
Tel. (9)57-47 98 19 - Fax (9)57-48 61 87
Sr Gonzalez Planton

Rooms 16 with air-conditioning, telephone, bath and WC. **Price** Single 3,500-5,150Pts, double 5,900-8,850Pts, triple 7,500-11,100Pts. **Meals** Breakfast 450Pts, served 8:00-10:00; half board + 1,500Pts, full board + 3,000Pts (per pers.). **Restaurant** Open from Mar to Oct; carte. Specialties: regional cooking **Credit cards** Amex, Visa, Eurocard, MasterCard. **Pets** Dogs not allowed. **Facilities** Garage (1.000Pts). **Nearby** Córdoba: Fiesta de los Patios (5-15 May); Feria de Nuestra Señora de Fuensanta (Sept.) - Medina Azahara(6km) - Monastery of San Jerónimo - Las Ermitas de Córdoba (13km) - Sanctuary of Santo Domingo de Scala Dei - Los Villares golf course (18-hole).**Open** All year.

The Gonzalez is a charming small hotel opened only a few years ago in an old house in the Juderia quarter close to the mosque. The white-marbled entrance, decorated with mirrors and impressive suspended copperwork, is imposing. The rooms are much more simple but nevertheless comfortable and are air-conditioned. You can choose between those giving onto the street or the quieter ones, which look onto the flowered patio.

How to get there (Map 19): in the old town.

Hostal Seneca *

14003 Córdoba
Calle Conde y Luque, 7
Tel. (9)57-47 32 34 - Sra Peignier

Rooms 12, 7 with bath and WC. **Price** Single 2,150-2,300Pts, double 4,000-4,250Pts, triple 7,250Pts. **Meals** Breakfast included, served 9:00-11:00. **Restaurant** See p. 194. **Credit cards** All major. **Pets** Dogs allowed. **Facilities** Parking (1.500Pts). **Nearby** Córdoba: Fiesta de los Patios (5-15 May); Feria de Nuestra Señora de Fuensanta (Sept.) - Medina Azahara(6km) - Monastery of San Jerónimo - Las Ermitas de Córdoba (13km) - Sanctuary of Santo Domingo de Scala Dei - Los Villares golf course (18-hole). **Open** 15-Jan - 15-Dec.

In the heart of old city, this small hotel is run by a very attractive French woman who, came here more than ten years ago after falling in love with Córdoba. Each year she sees the return of a loyal band of devotees won over by the atmosphere of calm and studied simplicity reigning here. Even if the comfort is less than perfect, you will feel relaxed and at ease in the nicely personalized rooms. Number 14 is recommended for its access to the terrace with its view over the roofs and minaret of the Mezquita close by. There is no restaurant but Number 8 on the same street is strongly recommended by the owner. A warm and relaxing ambiance is assured in this house with a soul all of its own.

How to get there *(Map 19): in the old town.*

Hotel la Bobadilla ★★★★★

18300 Loja (Granada)
Finca La Bobadilla - Apartado, 52
Tel. (9)58-32 18 61 - Fax. (9)58-32 18 10
Sra Uuartz

Rooms 60 with air-conditioning, telephone, bath, WC, cable TV and minibar; elevator. **Price** Single 21,600-26,800Pts, double 30,600-34,800Pts, suite 31,100-43,800Pts. **Meals** Breakfast included, served 8:00-11:00; half board + 5,200-6,400Pts. (per pers.). **Restaurant** Service 13:30-15:30, 20:30-23:00; "La Finca": carte 4,900-6,500Pts - "El Cortijo": carte: 2.100-4.600Pts. Specialties: regional and international cooking. **Credit cards** All major. **Pets** Dogs allowed only in the rooms. **Facilities** Swimming pool, tennis, riding, sauna, health center, garage. **Nearby** Loja - Los Infiernos de Lojas - Santa Fe - Granada. **Open** All year.

The Bobadilla is a 'grand luxe' hotel in a very beautiful residence built in the best Andalusian style, with succeeding patios, flowered terraces, gardens and fountains. The rooms are very comfortable and exquisitely decorated. The two restaurants serve a cuisine of quality. This hotel attracts with all that it offers for a truly relaxing stay: tennis court, a swimming pool, horse riding and a fitness center. All this is in a region not lacking in tourist interest, and note that very interesting reduced rates are available in the winter months (Christmas excepted), depending on length of stay.

How to get there *(Map 25): 76km east of Granada via N342; after Loja take road from Rute to Salinas, then private road.*

Alhambra Palace ★★★★

18009 Granada
Peña Partida 2, 4
Tel. (9)58-22 14 66/67/68 - Fax (9)58-22 64 04
Sr Hernandez Medina

Rooms 147 with air-conditioning, telephone, bath, WC, TV and minibar; elevator. **Price** Single 14,500Pts, double 18,500Pts, suite 21,500Pts. **Meals** Breakfast 1,200 Pts, served 7:30-10:00; half board + 5,400, full board 9,600Pts. (per pers.). **Restaurant** Service 13:00-15:30, 20:30-23:30; menu 4,125Pts, also à la carte. **Credit cards** All major. **Pets** Dogs allowed. **Facilities** Parking. **Nearby** Villages of Santa Fe, Fuentevaqueros, Valderrubio, Viznar (Federico Garcia Lorca National Park) - Guadix cathedral - Sierra Nevada. **Open** All year.

At the top of a small hill inside the Alhambra Gardens, the towers and minaret of this immense building dominate Granada and have a magnificent view from the terraces over the city and the year-round snow on the Sierra Nevada. The Moorish decoration, all blues and reds, the shining coppers and bronzes sometimes give the hotel a rather kitsch look; but in addition to the comfortable rooms, there are also nine luxury suites to benefit from such a sumptuous panorama. One also appreciates the 24-hour service in all rooms, the attention of the personnel and the private parking in a city with an almost full-time tourist presence. This is a good and beautiful hotel.

How to get there (Map 25): inside the Alhambra Gardens.

Hostal America ★

18009 Granada
Real de la Alhambra, 53
Tel. (9)58-22 74 71 – Fax (9)58-22 74 70
Sr Garzón

Rooms 14 with air-conditioning, telephone, bath, WC, and TV. **Price** Single 7,810-9,500Pts, double 12,410Pts, suite 17,015Pts. **Meals** Breakfast included, served 8:00-10:00; full board + 4,365Pts. (per pers. 3 days min.).**Restaurant** Service 13:00-15:00, 20:00-22:00; menu 2,000Pts, also à la carte. Specialties: Potajes al pujarreño - Cocidos - Platos de jamon - Serrano - Quesos manchegos. **Credit cards** All major. **Pets** Dogs not allowed. **Nearby** Villages of Santa Fe, Fuentevaqueros, Valderrubio, Viznar (Federico Garcia Lorca National Park) - Guadix cathedral - Sierra Nevada. **Open** 1. Mar-10. Nov.

It is inside the Real of the Alhambra that you will find the pretty white facade and flowered windows of the Hostal America. This modest but attractive place with its fourteen rooms has become a really charming hotel thanks to the care and talents of the owner. One is above all attracted by the relaxed atmosphere reigning here, and the place soon becomes intimate and almost familiar. The small size of the hotel, its simple but personalized decoration, the family cuisine and the warm welcome all mean a lot here and give its clients the impression of being guests in a friend's house. In summer meals are taken under the trellis in the green cool courtyard. One will always return here with pleasure.

How to get there (Map 25): inside the Alhambra.

Parador San Francisco ★★★★

18009 Granada
Real de la Alhambra
Tel. (9)58 22 14 40 - Fax (9)58 22 22 64
Sr Gianello Louro

Rooms 38 with air-conditioning, telephone, bath, WC, (14 with TV) and minibar. **Price** Single 17,810Pts, double 22,000-23,000Pts. **Meals** Breakfast 1,200 Pts, served 8:00-11:00; full board + 6,970Pts. (per pers. 2 days min.). **Restaurant** Service 13:00-16:00, 20:30-22:30; menu 3,500Pts, also à la carte. Specialties: Gazpacho - Tortilla de Sacramonte - Choto a l'alpurrena. **Credit cards** All major. **Pets** Dogs not allowed. **Facilities** Parking. **Nearby** Villages of Santa Fe, Fuentevaqueros, Valderrubio, Viznar (Federico Garcia Lorca National Park) - Guadix cathedral - Sierra Nevada. **Open** All year.

Set within the walls of the Alhambra, close to the Arab Alcazar and the palace of Charles V, the parador is housed in a former Franciscan convent founded by the Catholic Kings after the reconquest of the town. In the midst of the famous Alhambra Gardens, there is a superb view over the Generalife, the Albaicin and the Sierra Nevada. One has to wander through the galleries decorated with old Spanish furniture, in the patio and the chapel to be imbued with the serenity and beauty of this unique site. Ideal for idleness, a small Arab lounge recalls the origins of this site. Perfect for relaxation, the convent rooms are comfortable, while Numbers 205, 206 and 207 have terraces opening onto the Generalife. This Truly is a real "plus" in your discovery of Grenada; but be warned: 6-months advance reservation's are required in high season.

How to get there (Map 25): inside the Gardens of the Alhambra.

La Posada ★★★

18614 Gualchos (Granada)
Plaza de la Constitución, 3
Tel. (9)58-65 60 34 – Fax (9)58-65 60 34
Sr Gonzalez Zubiaurre

Rooms 9 with telephone, bath and WC. **Price** Double 5,000-10,000Pts. **Meals** Breakfast 800 Pts, served 9:00-11:00. **Restaurant** Service 13:00-15:30, 20:00-23:30; closed Mon; menus 3,100-4,200Pts, also à la carte. **Credit cards** Visa, Eurocard, MasterCard. **Pets** Dogs allowed. **Facilities** Swimming pool. **Nearby** Gualchos: the Torre Nueva - Church and castle of Castell de Ferro - Beaches of Castell de Ferro. **Open** 1. Mar - 30. Nov.

Off the classic tourist circuits of the Costa del Sol, Gualchos is a small village forgotten in the hills of the Sierra de Lujar. The inn was created out of three village houses, very cleverly merged together in an oasis of charm. The public rooms are furnished with great refinement and open and the charming swimming pool a verdant and flowered garden where breakfast may be taken. The bedrooms have a view of the village, the valley, or the sea. The cuisine is sophisticated and excellent and the prices are completely justified. Children of under 12 are not welcomed as the garden steps are considered too dangerous; the welcome could also be more friendly. Warning: access to the hotel is difficult as the roads are very narrow.

How to get there (Map 26): 90km south of Grenada via N323, then N340 towards Almeria.

Finca Buen Vino

21293 Los Marines (Huelva)
Tel. (9)59-12 40 34 - Fax (9)59-12 40 34
Sr et Sra Chesterton

Rooms 2 and 1 suite with bath and WC. **Price** half board single 12,000-15,000Pts, double 20,000-24,000Pts. **Meals** Breakfast included. **Restaurant** Evening meals; menu. Specialties: Spanish cooking. **Credit cards** Visa, Eurocard, MasterCard. **Pets** Dogs not allowed. **Facilities** Swimming pool (June-Sept), parking. **Nearby** Gruta de las Maravillas in Aracena (cave of Marvels) - Almonaster la Real - Church of the convent of Santa Clara in Moguer - Almonte - Isla Cristina - El Romero del Rocio of Huelva (May). **Open** 15. Jan - 15. Dec.

At equal distance from Lisbon and Gibraltar, and 50km from the border with Portugal, the Finca Buen Vino will prove a charming stopover for you. A residential hotel, you must reserve in advance if you wish to enjoy this pretty house with only three rooms open to visitors. The traditional Hispano-Moorish facade is overrun by roses and clematis. Bought a few years ago by an English couple, you will find full British charm and comfort in the interior: old furniture, chintzes, pot-pourri, souvenirs of the Empire, and so on. The same refinement is found around the guests' tables: linen napkins, silverware, crystal; all of it however arranged with a certain simplicity - even if correct dress is required for dinner. Midday meals are served on the terrace in summer. The kitchen garden, mixing flowers, vegetables and fruit supplies the house recipes. The welcome is cordial.

How to get there *(Map 26): 100km west of Seville via N431 towards Aracena.*

Parador Castillo de Santa Catalina ★★★★

23001 Jaén
Tel. (9)53-26 44 11 - Fax (9)53-26 44 11
Sr Huete

Rooms 45 with air-conditioning, telephone, bath, WC, TV and minibar. **Price** Double 13,000-14,000Pts. **Meals** Breakfast 1,100Pts, served 8:00-10:30; full board + 6,375Pts. (per pers. 2 days min.). **Restaurant** Service 13:00-16:00, 20:30-23:00; menu 3.200Pts, also à la carte. Specialties: regional cooking. **Credit cards** All major. **Pets** Dogs not allowed. **Facilities** Swimming pool, parking. **Nearby** In Jaén Feria de San Lucas (Oct) - Baeza - Ubeda - Martos. **Open** All year.

Attached to the impressive fortress built at the same period and in the same style as the Alhambra at Grenada, the Parador Santa Catalina has the severe appearance of a fortified castle with its stone outworks and the tiny apertures of its facade. The view however is superb over a valley scattered with olive groves. Most of the rooms have balconies and you can enjoy such a view at your leisure. The reception rooms are very spacious and have been arranged with furniture sometimes very much in the 1960's 'designer' style, and decorated with tapestries and canvasses on loan from various national museums. Do not miss the dining room with its lamps created in the spirit of Moorish-Arabic art.

How to get there *(Map 25): 4km west of Jaén.*

Hotel de la Perdíz ★★★

23200 La Carolina (Jaén)
Carret. N IV
Tel. (9)53-66 03 00 – Fax (9)53-68 13 62
Sr Felix Tasa

Rooms 95 with air-conditioning, telephone, bath, WC and TV. **Price** Single 8,300 Pts, double 11,500Pts. **Meals** Breakfast 800Pts, served 7:30-11:00; half board + 3,600Pts, full board + 5,500Pts. (per pers.). **Restaurant** Service 13:30-15:45, 20:45-23:15; menu 3,000Pts, also à la carte. Specialties: Game. **Credit cards** All major. **Pets** Dogs allowed in the rooms. **Facilities** Swimming pool, garage, parking. **Nearby** Convento de la Sierra Morena and Palacio de la Carolina - Feria (May). **Open** All year.

There is a very 'hunting lodge' ambiance in this hotel that owes its name to the park close by renowned for its abundant game. The large fireplaces, the hunting trophies and arms collections on the walls, the impressive beams of the ceiling and beautiful old Spanish furniture, all contribute to the warm and rustic atmosphere of the lounges. The bedrooms are more simple but are all carefully maintained and pleasant. At the heart of the building is a small enclosed garden planted with palm trees, scented cypresses and fig trees, which form a small haven of cool and peace. Most of the rooms have a view of the garden while others have terraces. If you cannot get one of these, go for those looking over the olive groves and the village.

How to get there (Map 19): *44km north of Linares via N322 until Bailén, then N4.*

Parador de Cazorla ★★★

Sacejo
23470 Cazorla (Jaén)
Tel. (9)53-72 70 75 - Fax (9)53-72 70 77

Rooms 33 with, telephone, bath and WC. **Price** Single 8,400-9,200Pts, double 10,500-11,500Pts. **Meals** Breakfast 1,100Pts, served 8:00-10:30; half board + 4,300Pts, full board + 6,375Pts. (per pers.). **Restaurant** Service 13:00-16:00, 20:30-22:30; menu 3,200Pts. Specialties: Game, trouts. **Credit cards** All major. **Pets** Dogs not allowed. **Facilities** Swimming pool, parking. **Nearby** Ubeda - Nature Park of Sierra de Cazorla: Embalse del Tranco and shores of the Guadalquivir - Quesada - Villages of the Sierra de Segura "Valle del Paraiso": Orcera, Beas de Segura and Segura de la Sierra. **Open** All year.

Arrival at the parador is already quite an expedition when one takes the mountain road at Cazorla leading to Sacejo. The trip is however worthwhile, both for the wild and wooded site but also for the picturesque villages that you drive through. One comes here above all for the walking, to fish or to hunt. The source of the Guadalquivir river is close by, and the Sierra de Cazorla is a very beautiful nature park scented by pines, oaktrees and junipers-the home of stags, deer and wild boar. The hotel architecture is inspired by the Andalusian 'cortijos', with care taken to look out over the surrounding nature as much as possible. This is why it is better to go for the rooms looking over the swimming pool side, as they have the best view. The decor is sober but all is comfortable and very well maintained. In the restaurant a cuisine favoring game is served, the specialty of the region. To better profit from the region, without worrying about the situation, do not hesitate to take part in the excursions (free) organized by the hotel for clients: cultural visits, horse riding or mountain bike trips, discovering the natural sites, among others-to get another view of Andalusia.

How to get there *(Map 20): 45km south of Ubeda; 25km east of Cazorla.*

Parador Condestable Davalos ★★★★

23400 Úbeda (Jaén)
Plaza Vasquez de Molina, 1
Tel. (9)53 75 03 45 - Fax (9)53 75 12 59
Sr Ronda

Rooms 31 with air-conditioning, telephone, bath, WC, TV and minibar. **Price** Single 11,600Pts, double 15,000Pts, suite 16,500Pts. **Meals** Breakfast 1,200Pts, served 8:00-10:30; half board + 3,200Pts, full board + 6,375Pts. (per pers.). **Restaurant** Service 13:00-16:00, 21:00-23:00; menu 3,200Pts. Specialties: Ajo blanco - Espiñacas al estilo Jaén - Pimientos rellenos de perdíz - Natillas con borrachuelos. **Credit cards** All major. **Pets** Dogs not allowed. **Facilities** Swimming pool, tennis, minigolf, sauna, parking. **Nearby** Sabiote - Nature Park of Sierra de Cazorla: Embalse del Tranco and shores of the Guadalquivir - Villanueva del Arrobispo - Jaén - Segura de la Sierra. **Open** All year.

This 16th-century palace boasts a long, Greco-Roman style facade in the historical part of the town, where a number of monuments from the Renaissance period rival its beauty. Renovated in the 18th century, it was converted into a hotel in 1942. The long glazed galleries, a dream patio where in summer a canopy is put up to create some cool, and bedrooms with a postcard view, all contribute to its delightful charm! To note: The suite on the facade forming the corner is very beautiful, and reasonably priced, while a 'taverne' on the ground floor will delight all lovers of good wines.

How to get there *(Map 20): 24km east of Linares via N322; next to the Salvador church and the Ayuntamiento (town hall).*

Parador del Golf ★★★★

29080 Málaga
Tel. (9)5-238 12 55 – Fax (9)5-238 21 41
Sr Garcia Alonso

Rooms 56 (and 4 suites with air-conditioning), telephone, bath, WC, TV and minibar. **Price** Single 10,600-11,870Pts, double 13,000-15,000Pts. **Meals** Breakfast 1,200Pts, served 8:00-10:30; full board + 6,375Pts. (per pers.). **Restaurant** Service 13:30-16:00, 20:30-23:00; menu 3,200Pts. **Credit cards** All major. **Pets** Dogs not allowed. **Facilities** Swimming pool, tennis, golf, parking. **Nearby** Beaches of Torremolinos - Cártama - Alora and Convento de Nuestra Señora Flores - Tropical gardens of the Hacienda de la Concepción (7km) - El Chorro and the Garganta del Chorro - Club Campo de Málaga golf course (18-hole). **Open** All year.

1 4km west of Málaga, the Parador del Golf will prove a stopping place particularly appreciated by adepts of this sport. On the golf course, the hotel is thus protected from the galloping urbanization that is ravaging the Costa del Sol. Access to the course is free for hotel guests from November 1 to June 30. Those not playing the game can always play tennis or unwind beside the large swimming pool or on the beach close by. The architecture is without much personality but has the merit of being discreet. The bedrooms are quiet and decorated with care. The service is irreproachable. Rather than a hotel of charm, here we have a 'de luxe' hotel to spoil all golfers.

How to get there *(Map 25): 14km west of Málaga.*

Parador Gibralfaro ★★★

Gibralfaro
29016 Málaga
Tel. (9)5-222 19 03 - Fax (9)5-222 19 04

Rooms 12 with air-conditioning, telephone, bath, WC, TV and minibar. **Price** Single 12,000Pts, double 15,000Pts, suite 21,000-27,000Pts. **Meals** Breakfast 1,200Pts, served 8:00-10:30; full board + 6,375Pts. (per pers.). **Restaurant** Service 13:00-16:00, 20:30-23:00; menu 3,200Pts, also à la carte. **Credit cards** All major. **Pets** Dogs not allowed. **Facilities** Parking. **Nearby** Beaches of Torremolinos - Cártama - Alora and Convento de Nuestra Señora Flores - Tropical gardens of the Hacienda de la Concepción (7km) - El Chorro and the Garganta del Chorro - Club Campo de Málaga golf course (18-hole). **Open** All year.

Situated on the Gibralfaro hill, the parador enjoys an uninterrupted view over the town and commercial port. The hotel has just a few comfortable and air-conditioned rooms, which is a considerable advantage in this part of Spain. Each room has its own terrace while the restaurant also has one, from which one can see the Malagueta quarter and the bullring. On a summer evening it is fun to linger at the bar and have a drink, while watching the lighted ships pass by. One also appreciates the beautiful walks in the gardens of the ancient fortress close to the hotel.

How to get there (Map 25): 3km from the center of Màlaga.

Trasierra

41370 Cazalla de la Sierra (Seville)
Tel. (9)54-88 43 24 – Fax (9)54-88 33 05
Sr et Sra Scott

Rooms 6 with bath and lounge. **Price** Double 12,000Pts (per pers.). **Meals** Breakfast included. **Restaurant** Evening meals by reservation – Service 13:00-16:00, 20:00-22:00; menu 3,500Pts. Specialties: regional cooking. **Credit cards** Amex, Visa, Eurocard, MasterCard. **Pets** Dogs not allowed. **Facilities** Swimming pool, parking. **Nearby** Seville, Còrdoba. **Open** All year.

R esidential hotels are not very common in Spain and the rare examples we have found are always homes opened by foreigners in love with this country. This is the case with Charlotte and Nick Scott who have restored a large olive oil mill and its outhouses in the Sierra Morena, about one hundred kilometers from Seville. This was a sizeable job and it needed all the passion of the owners and skills of the local workers to restore the spirit of the property. The bedrooms are vast and sober, decorated with travel souvenirs or traditional articles reworked in the neighboring village, which are also sold in the hotel's small boutique. The wild environment of the Sierra Morena is superb and your very welcoming hosts will be your best guides.

How to get there (Maps 18 & 24): 100km north of Seville.

La Fonda ★★★

29639 Benalmádena Pueblo (Málaga)
C/. Santo Domingo, 7
Tel. (9)5-256 82 73 – Fax (9)5-256 82 73
M. José Antonio Garcia

Rooms 28 with telephone, bath, WC (14 with TV). **Price** Single 4,000-6,500Pts, double 6,000-10.,000Pts, triple 7,500-11,500Pts. **Meals** Breakfast included **Restaurant** Service 13:00-15:00, closed Saturday, Sunday and National Holidays; menus and also à la carte. Specialties: regional and international cooking. **Credit cards** All major. **Pets** Dogs not allowed. **Facilities** Swimming pool, parking. **Nearby** Beaches of Marbella - Màlaga - Cártama - Alora and Convento de Nuestra Señora Flores - Tropical gardens of the Hacienda de la Concepción (7km) - El Chorro and the Garganta del Chorro - Club Campo de Málaga golf course (18-hole). **Open** All year.

Impossible to resist the charm of this hotel located at two paces from the ravishing little square of Benalmádena, where it is delightful to linger among the orange trees. Despite its proximity to the coast, only 4km away, the village dominates the surroundings and the Mediterranean, and has been preserved by some miracle. Built out of earlier houses, one is surprised to find no less than three different patios, one of them boasting the swimming pool. The purest Andalusian style, with the white of the walls set off by prettily arranged green plants and flowers, is highly attractive while the superb view of the sea only further emphasizes the architecture of the hotel. The most pleasant bedrooms are those enjoying this view.

How to get there *(Map 25): 20km south of Málaga, on the rapid highway Málaga-Cádiz, exit Benalmádena.*

Hotel Husa Mijas ★★★

29650 Mijas (Málaga)
Urbanizacion Tamisa, 2
Tel. (9)5-248 58 00 - Fax (9)5-248 58 25
Sr Martinez

Rooms 91 and 3 suites with telephone, bath, WC and TV. **Price** Single 8,000-12,000Pts, double 10,000-14,000Pts, suite 20,000-28,000Pts. **Meals** Breakfast 1,350Pts, served 7:30-10:30; half board + 4,150Pts, full board + 6,950Pts. (per pers.). **Restaurant** With air-conditioning; service 13:00-15:30, 20:00-22:30; menu 2,800Pts, also à la carte. **Credit cards** All major. **Pets** Dogs allowed in the rooms. **Facilities** Swimming pool, tennis (1,000Pts), sauna (1,000Pts), parking. **Nearby** Costa del Sol - Màlaga - Benalmàdena - Marbella - Club Campo de Málaga and Mijas golf course (18-hole). **Open** All year.

If you are afraid of the crowds on the over-visited Costa del Sol, but adore its sunshine and tanning all year round, you must make a trip up to the village of Mijas. Here on the small hills between Málaga and Marbella, among the pines and palm trees, with a view that cannot be taken away, is located the Mijas Hotel with a typically Andalusian character and a certain English spirit. The public rooms are sober but very comfortable, while the terraces promise delicious breakfasts in the shade of the olive trees, and are the ideal setting for summer dinners. The Mijas offers comfortable bedrooms but the suites are the most comfortable aven though only three have the best views. Two beautiful swimming pools, one heated throughout the year, a tennis court and a health center add to the attractions of this hotel.

How to get there *(Map 25): 30km southwest of Málaga via N340 towards Cádiz; at Fuengirola take small road for Mijas.*

Parador de Nerja ★★★★

29780 Nerja (Málaga)
Playa de Burriana
Tel. (9)5-252 00 50 – Fax (9)5-252 19 97
Sr Embiz Fabregas

Rooms 73 with air-conditioning, telephone, bath, WC, TV, minibar. **Price** Single 10,800Pts, double 14,500Pts. **Meals** Breakfast 1,200Pts, served 8:00-10:00; full board + 6,578Pts. (per pers.). **Restaurant** Service 13:00-15:30, 20:00-22:30; menus 3,200-3,500Pts, also à la carte. Specialties: Gazpacho - Frituras de pescados. **Credit cards** All major. **Pets** Dogs not allowed. **Facilities** Swimming pool, tennis, parking. **Nearby** Caverns of Nerja - Costa del Sol - Màlaga - Club Campo de Málaga golf course (18-hole). **Open** All year.

Nerja is a tourist town on a high cliff overlooking the Costa del Sol, at the foot of which stretch away beaches of fine sand. This is said to be 'the balcony of Europe' from where one can enjoy a splendid panorama of the sea and the high sierras surrounding it. The parador can also be proud of its superb view. It dominates the beach of Burriana which can be reached directly by elevator. In the bedrooms offer excellent comfort, and almost all of them have balconies and are fitted with beautiful bathrooms. One rather regrets however a somewhat impersonal decor that deserves more care. In the lawned garden are the bar and swimming pool. Here you can enjoy the calm of the site in the shade of the Bella Sombra, some very beautiful trees that serve as sun-umbrellas. For a more pleasant stay, come here out of season.

How to get there *(Map 25): 51km east of Málaga via N340.*

Refugio de Juanar ★★★

29610 Ojén (Málaga)
Tel. (9)5-288 10 00 - Fax (9)5-288 10 01
Sr Gomez Avila

Rooms 25 with telephone, bath, WC, TV and minibar. **Price** Single 6,800-7,200Pts, double 8,400-9,300Pts, suite 10,950-16.400Pts, 4 pers. 13,550-14,500Pts, appart. for 6 pers. 24,900-27,500Pts. **Meals** Breakfast 825Pts, served 8:30-11:00; half board + 3,200Pts, full board + 7,400Pts. (per pers.). **Restaurant** Service 13:00-16:00, 20:00-22:30; menu 2,800Pts, also à la carte. Specialties: Game. **Credit cards** All major. **Pets** Dogs not allowed. **Facilities** Swimming pool, tennis, parking. **Nearby** Marbella Coìn - Alozaina - Ronda. **Open** All year.

A parador in other times, this hotel has now been taken over by its employees. Starting from Ojen, take a small mountain road leading to the Sierra de Ronda, a major center for hunting the 'capra hispanica', as well as smaller game (partridges, rabbits, etc.). Hidden in this superb countryside is this former property of the Marquis de Tarios, a favorite hunting ground of King Alfonso XVIII. This is a comfortable mountain hotel where an ambiance of warmth reigns, and where a good cuisine based on game is available. For the bedrooms, our favorite is Number 3, in which General de Gaulle completed the writing of his memoirs !

How to get there (Map 25): 65km southwest of Málaga via N340 to Marbella, then continue via C337; 10km after Ojén.

Marbella Club Hotel ★★★★

29600 Marbella (Málaga)
Bd. Principe Alfonso Von Hohenlohe
Tel. (9)5-282 22 11 - Fax (9)5-282 98 84
Sr Wollner

Rooms 100 with air-conditioning, telephone, bath, WC, cable TV and minibar. **Price** Single 20,000-39,500Pts, double 24,000-42,000Pts, suite 38,500-55,000Pts. **Meals** Breakfast 1,800Pts (buffet), served 8:30-10:30; half board + 7,700Pts, full board + 10,900Pts. (per pers.). **Restaurant** Service from 20:00; menu 5,500Pts, also à la carte. Specialties: regional and international cooking. **Credit cards** All major. **Pets** Dogs not allowed. **Facilities** Swimming pool, beach, tennis, health center, sauna, parking. **Nearby** Costa del Sol - Ojén - Coìn - Rio Real los Monteros golf course (18-hole), Nueva Andalucia golf course (18-hole). **Open** All year.

In a magnificent and faultlessly maintained garden, the Marbella Club Hotel's bungalows assure complete privacy and unmatched comfort. The impeccable decor matches the image of the place, luxurious and refined. Bathrooms in marble, coordinated printed fabrics—nothing is left to chance. Those Hollywood stars coming here to find relaxation in line with their standing will not be disappointed. Besides the fully equiped beach and the beautiful swimming pool, all the services wished for are assured, to guarantee a 'de luxe' and charming stay.

How to get there *(Map 25): 56km southwest of Málaga via N340.*

Puente Romano ★★★★★

29600 Marbella (Málaga)
Tel. (9)5-282 09 00 - Fax (9)5-277 57 66
Sr Jean-Louis Dulau - Sr Palaso

Rooms 185 with air-conditioning, telephone, bath, WC, cable TV, safe and minibar. **Price** Single 17,400-30,000Pts, double 22,100-40,000Pts, suite 27,900-45,000Pts. **Meals** Breakfast 1,700-2,100Pts (buffet), served 8:00-11:00; half board + 6,800-7,200Pts, full board + 10,100P-14,000Pts. (per pers.). **Restaurant** Service 13.00-16.00, 20:00-24.00; menus 3,950-5,850Pts, also à la carte. Specialties: regional and international cooking. **Credit cards** All major. **Pets** Small dogs allowed in the room and in the garden. **Facilities** Swimming pool, tennis, health center, sauna, parking. **Nearby** Costa del Sol - Ojén - Coin - Rio Real los Monteros golf course (18-hole), Nueva Andalucia golf course (18-hole). **Open** All year.

A 'grande luxe' hotel, the Puente Romano sports its five stars with serenity and without ostentation. With its elegant Andalusian architecture (unfortunately beside a busy national road), the hotel is made up of small bungalows in an admirable garden of exquisite freshness. The contemporary decor is luxurious but in good taste and the super-abundance of equipment of all sorts (3 swimming pools, a gym, 3 restaurants, private beach, etc.), and the quality of service will satisfy even the most demanding. This is a true oasis in the surrounding mediocrity of the region; a true establishment of charm and luxury.

How to get there (Map 25): 56km southwest of Málaga via N340.

Hotel Reina Victoria ★★★★

29400 Ronda (Málaga)
Tel. (9)5-287 12 40 – Fax (9)5-287 10 75
Sra Caballero

Rooms 87 and 2 suites with air-conditioning, telephone, bath, WC and TV; elevator. **Price** Single 8,500-9,800Pts, double 13,000-15,000Pts, suite 19,000-23,000Pts. **Meals** Breakfast 1,300Pts, served 7:45-10:45. **Restaurant** Service 13:00-15:30, 20:00-22:00; carte. Specialties: regional and international cooking. **Credit cards** All major. **Pets** Small dogs allowed. **Facilities** Swimming pool, parking. **Nearby** Setenil - Alozaina - Serriana de Ronda via San Pedro de Alcántara - Grazalema - Road from Ronda to Ubrique - Feria of Ronda (May). **Open** All year.

One can understand why the Austrian poet made the Hotel Reina Victoria his favorite vacation resort. This spot is romantic to excess and has everything to exalt even the most blasé personalities. The town is perched on a rocky spur traversed by the spectacular gorges of the Rio Tajo, and has several architectural treasures. The traditional habitat of chalk-whited houses has been preserved with great care. As for the surrounding country environment, it is quite simply superb. The ultimate of superlatives, opt for a 'room with a view' from Numbers 105 to 124, or 205 to 222, or—even better—305 to 307, and enjoy the full magic of the place and its splendid panorama. The hotel's decor is a little faded but also completely charming. The rooms are large enough and decorated with old prints, and all are very peaceful. Some however would merit from a little refurbishing if the hotel does not intend to become a literary souvenir.

How to get there (Map 24): 96km north of Algeciras via C331, then C341.

36

Hotel Alfonso XIII *****

41004 Seville
San Fernando, 2
Tel. (9)5-422 28 50 - Fax (9)5-421 60 33
Sr Hamburger

Rooms 149 with air-conditioning, telephone, bath, WC, cable TV and minibar; elevator. **Price** Single 28,000-45,000Pts, double 38,000-56,000Pts, suite 82,000-150,000Pts. **Meals** Breakfast 2,400Pts, served 7:00-12:00; half board + 9,400Pts (per pers.). **Restaurant** Service 13:00-15:30, 20:30-23:30; menu 7,000Pts, also à la carte. Specialties: regional and international cooking. **Credit cards** All major. **Pets** Dogs not allowed. **Facilities** Parking and garage (2.000Pts). **Nearby** Cantillana - Carmona - Alcala de Guadaira - Sanlúcar la Mayor - Convento de San Isidoro del Campo in Santiponce and ruins of the Roman colony of Itàlica - Romero de Rocio of Huelva (May) - Semana Santa (Holy week in March) and the April Fair (May) ; Golf e Hipodromo del Club Pineda golf course (9-Hole). **Open** All year.

The Alfonso XIII was built to receive leading visitors to the Hispano-American Exhibition in 1929, and since then it has continued as a luxury hotel linked to the very history of Seville. The work of the architect Espinau-Munoz, who insisted that the hotel should truly represent the city, he designed it as a major Hispano-Moorish palace. The building is set around a large central patio surrounded by a glazed gallery, with arches deployed above white marble columns. Gardens planted with tropical vegetation surround the four facades of the palace. Sumptuous lounges follow each other in succession; while the bedrooms are perfect, we would have preferred if they gave onto the garden.

How to get there *(Map 24): alongside the cathedral.*

Hotel Doña Maria ★★★★

41004 Seville
Don Remondo, 19
Tel. (9)5-422 49 90 - Fax (9)5-421 95 46
Sr Rodriguez Andrade

Rooms 61 with air-conditioning, telephone, bath, WC, TV and safe; elevator. **Price** Single 7,000-16,000Pts, double 12,000-29,000Pts. **Meals** Breakfast 1,300Pts, served 8:00-11:00. **Restaurant** See pp. 196-197. **Credit cards** All major. **Pets** Dogs not allowed. **Facilities** Swimming pool on the roof, parking (1,200Pts). **Nearby** Cantillana - Carmona - Alcala de Guadaira - Sanlúcar la Mayor - Convento de San Isidoro del Campo in Santiponce and ruins of the Roman colony of Itàlica - Romero de Rocio of Huelva (May) - Semana Santa (Holy week in March) and the April Fair (May) ; Golf e Hipodromo del Club Pineda golf course (9-Hole). **Open** All year.

In the heart of the city, the Hotel Doña Maria is of recent construction. Nonetheless, the arcades of the interior architecture, the wrought iron work, the old furniture and the ravishing patio with its exuberant and exotic plants, all give it a very Andalusian character. The bedrooms are all personalized and beautiful, but Room 310, all white with lace and a canopied bed, gets our top vote as it also has a balcony opening onto the square, the orange trees and the cathedral. However, the supreme luxury of this hotel is the swimming pool on the roof, with the tower of the Giralda rising beside it just a few meters away. This is one of the best accommodetions in Seville.

How to get there (Map 24): next to the cathedral, facing the Giralda.

Hotel Los Seises ★★★★

41004 Seville
Calle Segovias, 6
Tel. (9)5-422 94 95 - Fax. (9)5-422 43 34 - Sr Reinoso

Rooms 43 with air-conditioning, telephone, bath, WC, cable TV, safe and minibar; elevator. **Price** Single 13,000-21,000Pts, double 16,000-25,000Pts. **Meals** Breakfast 1,500Pts, served 8:00-10:30; half board + 6,600Pts, full board + 10,000Pts (per pers.). **Restaurant** Service 13.30-15.30, 20.30-23.00; carte. Specialties: international and regional cooking. **Credit cards** All major. **Pets** Dogs not allowed. **Facilities** Swimming pool on the roof, parking. **Nearby** Cantillana - Carmona - Alcala de Guadaira - Sanlúcar la Mayor - Convento de San Isidoro del Campo in Santiponce and ruins of the Roman colony of Itàlica - Romero de Rocio of Huelva (May) - Semana Santa (Holy week in Mar.) and the April Fair (May); Golf e Hipodromo del Club Pineda golf course, (9-Hole). **Open** All year.

Los Seises is a 'de luxe' hotel of very unique design in the heart of Seville. By adapting a 16th-century palace into a hotel, numerous more ancient remnants were found and conserved in this 'neo-art deco' style, with its very pure lines. Thus one comes across a Roman mosaic, an Arab well and 16th-century marble columns, among other discoveries. The bedrooms are very elegant with their beds harmonizing with the light-colored walls and terra-cotta tiled floors. Without useless knick-knacks, one easily feels at home, while certain rooms can be surprising–such as Number 219, traversed by an ancient stone arch that gives an astonishing contrast. The last surprise is, the hotel roof, which transformed into a large terrace with a view of the roofs of the town; it also has a swimming pool, an inestimable attraction in Seville. At weekends the hotel offers very interesting rates, so do not hesitate as Los Seises is well worth the trouble.
How to get there (Map 24): near to the Giralda.

Taberna del Alabadero ★★★★

41001 Seville
Calle Zaragozas, 20
Tel. (9)5-456 06 37 - Fax (9)5-456 36 66
M. Jesus Raza

Rooms 7 with air-conditioning, telephone, bath, WC, cable TV, safe and minibar; elevator. **Price** Double 15,000-22,000Pts. **Meals** Breakfast included. **Restaurant** Service 13.30-15.30, 20.30-23.00; carte 4,100-7,000Pts. Specialties: Basque and Andalusian cooking. **Credit cards** All major. **Pets** Dogs not allowed. **Facilities** garage (1,750Pts). **Nearby** Cantillana - Carmona - Alcala de Guadaira - Sanlúcar la Mayor - Convento de San Isidoro del Campo in Santiponce and ruins of the Roman colony of Itàlica - Romero de Rocio of Huelva (May) - Semana Santa (Holy week in March) and the April Fair (May); Golf e Hipodromo del Club Pineda golf course (9-Hole). **Open** All year except in Aug.

Right in the heart of the Andalusian capital, close to the famous Real Maestranza bullring and the Santa Cruz quarter, here is found the Taberna del Alabadero. This 19th-century house formerly belonged to the Spanish poet José Antoine Cavestany, before becoming a well-known restaurant famed for its Basque-Andalusian cuisine. To add perfection to all this, a few bedrooms have been opened, all luxurious, very refined and very comfortable. Some look onto the typical Sevillian narrow streets, others onto the patio. As so often, everything radiates out from the large hallway on the ground floor, filled with the splashing sounds from the refreshing fountain and lit by a large glazed roof. This is the heart of the house and it is here that one can take a meal or a glass at the bar, as this is a beautiful address.

How to get there *(Map 24): in the Arenal district.*

Hotel San Gil ★★★

41002 Seville
Calle Parras, 28
Tel. (9)5-490 68 11 - Fax (9)5-490 69 39

Rooms 35 with air-conditioning, telephone, bath, WC, TV and minibar; elevator. **Price** Single 10,400-15,300Pts, double-duplex 12,000-19,600Pts, suite 18,200-25,200Pts. **Meals** Breakfast 800Pts, served 7:00-11:00. **Restaurant** See pp.196-197. **Credit cards** All major. **Pets** Dogs not allowed. **Facilities** Swimming pool. **Nearby** Cantillana - Carmona - Alcala de Guadaira - Sanlúcar la Mayor - Convento de San Isidoro del Campo in Santiponce and ruins of the Roman colony of Itàlica - Romero de Rocio of Huelva (May) - Semana Santa (Holy week in Mar) and the April Fair (May) ; Golf e Hipodromo del Club Pineda golf course (9-Hole). **Open** All year.

The Hotel San Gil has only recently opened in the center of Seville, in an old building with a loggia and balconies in wrought iron, framed by two more recent wings that respect the traditional architecture. The entry, reception and elevator areas are abundantly decorated with a patchwork of colored ceramics in the Moorish style, and the lounges are in this older part of the building. The bedrooms are in the windowed building surrounding the interior garden with its inevitable fountain. Most are in duplex-style or apartments with well-equipped kitchens for a longer stay. One finds pastel colors with a mix of modern and older-style furniture, along with well-appointed bathrooms, and all ensure full comfort. The swimming pool on the roof is also a major attraction for those visiting southern Spain in the summer. This is definitely 'algo mas que un hotel" ("more than just a hotel"), as the brochure tells us.

How to get there (Map 24): *close the Arco de Macapena.*

Las Casas de la Juderia ★★★

41004 Seville
Callejon de dos Hermanas, 7
Tel. (9)5-441 51 50 - Fax (9)5-442 21 70

Appartments 30 with air-conditioning, telephone, bath, WC, TV and kitchen. **Price** 1 pers. 9,000-15,000Pts, 2 pers. 11,500-19,000Pts, 3-4 pers. 15,500-25,000Pts. **Meals** Breakfast 1,100Pts, served 7:30-11:30. **Restaurant** See pp.196-197. **Credit cards** All major. **Pets** Dogs not allowed. **Facilities** Parking (500-1.000Pts). **Nearby** Cantillana - Carmona - Alcala de Guadaira - Sanlúcar la Mayor - Convento de San Isidoro del Campo in Santiponce and ruins of the Roman colony of Itàlica - Romero de Rocio of Huelva (May) - Semana Santa (Holy week in Mar.) and the April Fair (May) ; Golf e Hipodromo del Club Pineda golf course (9-Hole). **Open** All year.

In the real heart of historic Seville, Las Casas de la Juderia is a very old private hotel transformed into suites of one, two or three rooms. Long stays are possible here as most suites have a kitchen. The architecture of the place is really exceptional, with numerous flowered patios made pleasant by fountains, so that one can enjoy some peace and quiet in the shade of the arcades. The quality refurbishing of this house does not stop at the exterior and a real effort has been made to decorate the rooms (all different) with old furniture or quality reproductions. Finally, you can go up on the terraces with their view over the city roofs. The personnel are friendly and this is a stopping place of real charm.

How to get there (Map 24): in the historic center of the town.

La Rábida ★★

41001 Seville
Castelar, 24
Tel. (9)5-422 09 60 - Fax (9)5-422 43 75

Rooms 100 with air-conditioning, telephone, bath or shower, WC, cable TV; elevator. **Price** Single 5,000-8,000Pts, double 8,000-12,250Pts; full board 14,000-19.250Pts (per 2 pers., 3. days min.). **Meals** Breakfast 450Pts, served 7:30-10:30. **Restaurant** Service 13:00-15:00, 20:00-22:00; menu 1,815Pts. **Credit cards** All major. **Pets** Dogs not allowed. **Facilities** parking (500-1.000Pts). **Nearby** Cantillana - Carmona - Alcala de Guadaira - Sanlúcar la Mayor - Convento de San Isidoro del Campo in Santiponce and ruins of the Roman colony of Itàlica - Romero de Rocio of Huelva (May) - Semana Santa (Holy week in Mar) and the April Fair (May) ; Golf e Hipodromo del Club Pineda golf course (9-Hole). **Open** All year.

Even though it is in the historic center of Seville, close to the cathedral, La Rábida is a comfortable hotel; the reception is welcoming and the rooms are well furnished. The welcome and service are efficient. Apart from the historical and artistic interest of the city itself, the capital of Andalusia, Seville organizes each year two major events, Holy Week and 'La Feria', which attract a large number of tourists from around the world. This is why it is so difficult to find lodgings and one can only recommend that reservations be made as soon as possible.

How to get there (Map 24): in the city center.

Hotel Residencia Sevilla ★★

41003 Seville
Calle Daòiz, 5
Tel. (9)5-438 41 61 - Fax (9)5-490 21 60
M. José Arenas

Rooms 38 with air-conditioning, telephone, bath or shower, WC; elevator. **Price** Single 3,000-6,500Pts, double 5,000-10,000Pts. **Meals** No breakfast. **Restaurant** See pp. 196-197. **Credit cards** Amex, Visa, Eurocard, MasterCard. **Pets** Dogs allowed. **Facilities** Parking (1.000-1.500Pts). **Nearby** Cantillana - Carmona - Alcala de Guadaira - Sanlúcar la Mayor - Convento de San Isidoro del Campo in Santiponce and ruins of the Roman colony of Itàlica - Romero de Rocio of Huelva (May) - Semana Santa (Holy week in Mar) and the April Fair (May); Golf e Hipodromo del Club Pineda golf course (9-Hole). **Open** All year.

This is a small and unpretentious hotel, a very precious staging post in Seville. The hotel is on a charming and very quiet square scented by the orange trees lining it. The hotel offers a pretty flowered patio and simple but comfortable rooms, and a central location that speaks in its own favor. No breakfast is served but the attractive bar opposite will make it their pleasure to welcome you.

How to get there *(Map 24): in the city center via Sierpes street.*

Hotel Simon ★

41001 Seville
Garcia de Vinuesa, 19
Tel. (9)5-422 66 60 – Fax (9)5-456 22 41 – Sr Aguayo

Rooms 29 with telephone, bath or shower and WC. **Price** Single 4,500-6,000Pts, double 6,000-9,500Pts, suite 9,000-13,000Pts. **Meals** Breakfast 400Pts, served 8:00-10:30; half board + 2,200Pts, full board +4,000Pts (per pers. 2 days min.). **Restaurant** Service 13:00-15:00, 20:30-22:00; closed Tues; menu 1,800Pts, also à la carte. Specialties: regional and international cooking. **Credit cards** All major. **Pets** Dogs not allowed. **Facilities** Parking and garage (2.000Pts). **Nearby** Cantillana - Carmona - Alcala de Guadaira - Sanlúcar la Mayor - Convento de San Isidoro del Campo in Santiponce and ruins of the Roman colony of Itàlica - Romero de Rocio of Huelva (May) - Semana Santa (Holy week in Mar) and the April Fair (May); Golf e Hipodromo del Club Pineda golf course (9-Hole). **Open** All year.

Very well situated and only a few paces from the Giralda, the Alcazar and the Santa Cruz quarter, the hotel is in a typically Sevillian house (end-18th, early-19th century) adapted to the hotel requirements but still keeping its own special atmosphere. The dining room, lounge and bedrooms are cosy with a rather baroque luxury: ceramic-covered walls, pendant lamps, religious pictures, mirrors with gilded wood frames, etc.. The patio arranged as lounge is a very cool area: a fountain surrounded by ferns, along with a romantic sculpted bust, give it a most charming aspect. Its situation and its good price/value relationship make it very popular, and reservations should be made well in advance.

How to get there (Map 24): near the cathedral.

Hotel Oromana ★★★

41500 Alcala de Guadaira (Seville)
Avenida de Portugal
Tel. (9)5-568 64 00 - Fax (9)5-568 64 00
Clara Campoamor

Rooms 30 with air-conditioning, telephone, bath, WC and TV. **Price** Single 7,700-14,200Pts, double 10,200-14,200Pts. **Meals** Breakfast included, served 8:00-11:00. **Restaurant** Service 13:30-15:30, 20:00-23:00; carte 2,000-3,000Pts. Specialties: Croquelos de Ave - Arroz caldoso con Gambas. **Credit cards** All major. **Pets** Dogs not allowed. **Facilities** Swimming pool, parking. **Nearby** Gandul - Seville - Carmona - Sanlùcar la Mayor ; Convento de San Isidoro del Campo in Santiponce and ruins of the Roman colony of Itàlica - Romero de Rocio of Huelva (May) - Semana Santa of Sevilla (Holy week in Mar) and the April Fair (May); Golf e Hipodromo del Club Pineda golf course (9-Hole). **Open** All year.

A group of very attractive Andalusian women have just taken over the hotel and have doted it with a shared name: Clara Campoamor. Nobody doubts that they will succeed in their undertaking, and at 14km from Seville this hotel will well suit those looking for some peace, and the cool and fresh air of the evening. The Hotel Oromana is in fact in a wooded park not far from the river Guadaira which is lined with old Arab mills. A real example of Andalusian architecture, it attracts from the very first view. Inside its intimate decoration gives it the air of a family home, and all the rooms are attractive with their comfort and view of the countryside. The special gentleness of the welcome, the very reasonable prices and the ease of parking will perhaps make you prefer this hotel.

How to get there (Map 24): 14km southeast of Seville via N334; in the pine woods of Oromana.

Hotel Hacienda San Ygnacio ★★★★

41950 Castilleja de la Cuesta (Seville)
Calle Real, 194
Tel. (9)5-416 04 30 - Fax (9)5-416 14 37

Rooms 16 with air-conditioning, telephone, bath, WC, TV and minibar. **Price** Single 7,000-13,000Pts, double 10,000-16,000Pts, suite 45,000-65,000Pts. **Meals** Breakfast included, served 8:00-11:00. **Restaurant** "Almazara" Service 13:30-15:30, 20:00-23:00; closed Sun; carte 4,000-5.,000Pts. Specialties: regional cooking. **Credit cards** All major. **Pets** Dogs not allowed. **Facilities** Swimming pool, tennis. **Nearby** Gandul - Seville - Cantillana - Carmona - Alcala de Guadaira - Sanlúcar la Mayor - Convento de San Isidoro del Campo in Santiponce and ruins of the Roman colony of Itàlica - Romero de Rocio of Huelva (May) - Semana Santa of Sevilla (Holy week in Mar) and the April Fair (May); Golf e Hipodromo del Club Pineda golf course (9-Hole). **Open** All year.

Only 6 kilometers from Seville, this is a good formula for those bold enough to visit southern Spain in summertime. They will find peace and quiet here and can pass the hottest hours of the day beside the swimming pool, before setting off on an excursion. The hotel is a former 'hacienda' that has retained its architecture intact – a variety of buildings with a mixture of roofs, chimneys, terraces, bell-towers, all enclosing a large central courtyard planted with four superb palm trees. The large dining room of the 'Almazara', in the former mill of the 'hacienda', gives straight onto this beautiful patio. There are not many rooms and they are sober, decorated with wrought iron beds and rustic furniture, but all are spacious and comfortable. The swimming pool is in a green corner of the garden, surrounded by palm and orange trees.

How to get there *(Map 24) : 6km northwest of Seville via A49, towards Huelva, exit 3.*

Casa de Carmona ★★★★★

41410 Carmona (Seville)
Plaza de Lasso
Tel. (9)5-414 33 00 – Fax (9)5-414 37 52 – Sra F. Merina

Rooms 30 with air-conditioning, telephone, bath, WC, cable TV, safe and minibar; elevator. **Price** Single 22,000-34,000Pts, double 26,000-39,000Pts, 3 pers. 31,000-46,000Pts. **Meals** Breakfast 1,500Pts, served from 7:15; half board + 8,000Pts, full board + 9,700Pts. (per pers.). **Restaurant** Service 12:30-16:00, 19:00-24:00; menu 4,000Pts, also à la carte. Specialties: regional cooking. **Credit cards** All major. **Pets** Dogs not allowed. **Facilities** Swimming pool, fitness club, sauna, parking (2.000Pts). **Nearby** Church Santa Maria, Roman Necropolis (Elephant Vault, Servilia Tomb...), in Carmona - Fuentes de Andalucia - Seville - Convento de San Isidoro del Campo in Santiponce and ruins of the Roman colony of Itàlica - Romero de Rocio of Huelva (May) - Semana Santa of Sevilla (Holy week in Mar) and the April Fair (May); Golf e Hipodromo del Club Pineda golf course (9-Hole). **Open** All year.

Just a few kilometers from Seville, the ancient Andalusian city of Carmona shelters one of the most luxurious hotels of charm in Spain. Opened in 1991, the Casa de Carmona is a former palace furbished with a luxury of refinements. The public rooms are remarkable; the admirable patio with its flowery pot plants gives a tone to the entrance; and two lounge-conference rooms decorated with portraits of aristocrats and ancient livery all give you the impression of being received by some Spanish grandee. The small swimming pool is ravishing and allows you to freshen up in the shade of the marble columns. All the rooms are different and each has its own personality via a subtle mix of old furniture and coordinated pastel shades and fabrics. We recommend Number 6 for its admirable ceiling of Andalusian caissons, but also Numbers 14 and 18 for their views over the town. The varied and attentive personnel are discreet and perfect.
How to get there (Map 24): *33km east of Seville via N4, towards Córdoba.*

48

Hotel Cortijo Aguila Real ★★★★

41210 Guillena (Seville)

Tel. (9)55-578 50 06 – Fax (9)55-578 43 30 – Mme Martinez

Rooms 8 and 3 suites with air-conditioning, telephone, bath, WC, TV. **Price** Single 15,000Pts, double 20,000Pts. **Meals** Breakfast 1,250Pts, served 8:00-11:00; half board + 4,500Pts, full board + 7,000Pts. (per pers.). **Restaurant** Service 13:45-16:00, 20:15-22:30; menu 3,500Pts, also à la carte. Specialties: Game. **Credit cards** All major. **Pets** Small dogs allowed. **Facilities** Swimming pool, parking. **Nearby** Seville - Cantillana - Carmona - Alcala de Guadaira - Convento de San Isidoro del Campo in Santiponce and ruins of the Roman colony of Itàlica - Romero de Rocio of Huelva (May) - Semana Santa of Sevilla (Holy week in Mar) and the April Fair (May); Golf e Hipodromo del Club Pineda golf course (9-Hole). **Open** All year.

At some twenty kilometers from Seville one arrives at Cortigo Aguila Real via a road lined with fields of wheat and sunflowers, and arid land. Little by little, like some oasis in the desert, one begins to see the Cortigo on the summit of its hill. It is a former farm and the farm buildings surrounding the large courtyard have been arranged to give great independence to visitors. The rooms are very spacious and fitted with regional furniture, while three also have open fireplaces. All are perfectly comfortable and impeccably maintained. Meals can be taken either in the dining room, on the terrace or in the shade of the pine trees beside the swimming pool, from where one has a very splendid view over the plain with Seville in the distance. A same flexibility with the menus, which you can amend as you wish. Game, fresh and natural produce are the basics of the cuisine served. The hotel organizes bullfighting demonstrations in the ring on the property, as well as horse riding trips or tourist visits. Peace and quiet and a very warm welcome make this hotel an admirable address.

How to get there (Map 24): 20km north of Seville via E803, towards Merida; at Guillena (after the Itàlica ruins, road to the right between tow gas station), then towards Burguillos.

Hacienda Benazuza ★★★★

41800 Sanlùcar La Mayor (Seville)
Tel. (9)55-70 33 44 - Fax (9)55-70 34 10 - Sr Elejabeitia

Rooms 44 suites with air-conditioning, telephone, bath, WC, cable TV and minibar. **Price** Single 26,400-40,000Pts, double 33,000-50,000Pts, suite 45,000-65,000Pts. **Meals** Breakfast 1,500-3,500Pts, served 8:00-11:00; half board + 6,500Pts, full board + 10,500Pts. (per pers.). **Restaurant** "La Alqueira" and "El Patio" service 13:15-16:00, 20:15-22:30; carte 8,000Pts, "La Alberca" (swimming pool) carte 7,000Pts. **Credit cards** All major. **Pets** Dogs allowed. **Facilities** Swimming pool, tennis, paddle tennis, putting green, parking. **Nearby** Seville - Cantillana - Carmona - Alcala de Guadaira - Convento de San Isidoro del Campo in Santiponce and ruins of the Roman colony of Itàlica - Semana Santa (Holy week in Mar) - Rocio de Sanlucar (May); Golf e Hipodromo del Club Pineda golf course (9-Hole). **Open** All year.

A new grand hotel of charm has just opened in the Sevillian Aljarafe (High Ground). Both Arab and Andalusian, the Hacienda Benazuza groups different buildings constructed across the centuries. The surrounding wall reminds one of its Saracen origins in the 10th century, while the tower above the entry postern carries the coat of arms granted to the Counts of Benazuza in the 16th century. Most careful work in the archives has given its original splendor back to the Hacienda. The walls have refound their ocre, red, yellow and orange colors, the lounges their mudejar ceilings and the floorings of terra-cotta and enamelled tiles. The rooms and their bathrooms are superb even though one would have preferred that they continue in the Hispano-Moorish style. In the restaurants one discovers both Mediterranean and Oriental flavors. The small Hacienda chapel plays an active part in Holy Week and the 'Rocio de Sanlucar La Mayor': you will be well placed to enjoy these events, some of the most important in Andalusian culture.

How to get there *(Map 24): 33km west of Seville via N431, towards Huelva.*

50

Hotel Albarracín ★★★

44100 Albarracín (Teruel)
Azagra
Tel. (9)78-71 00 11 - Fax (9)78-60 53 63
Sr Cubo Sebastian

Rooms 14 with telephone, bath, WC and TV. **Price** Single 5,675-6,700Pts, double 10,500-12,045Pts. **Meals** Breakfast included, served 8:30-10:30; half board + 2,750Pts (per pers.). **Restaurant** Service 13:00-16:00, 20:30-22:30; menu 1,500Pts, also à la carte. Specialties: Migas con uvas - Jamón de Teruel - Cordero al horno - Codornices estofados - Ciervo - Jabali - Melocotón al vino. **Credit cards** All major. **Pets** Dogs allowed in rooms. **Facilities** Swimming pool, parking. **Nearby** in Abarracín: San Salvador Cathedral (Flemish Tapestries) - Callejon del Plou and Abrigo del Navazo (Prehistoric painting) - Teruel. **Open** All year.

A sort of fortified castle in a small historically classified village–this is the Hotel Albarracín. The interior has been modernized but not always in the best taste, but the splendid staircase has been preserved, as have the beams of the ancient building. The bedrooms are very neat and furnished in the Aragonese style. From the hotel one can gaze out on the countryside with the narrow lanes and small squares, its gentle hills, while the location is so quiet that only bird song risks waking you. The village is fun to discover, with its houses and their wooden balconies, some of them leaning outwards astonishingly, all so typically Spanish !

How to get there (Map 14): 45km west of Teruel.

Parador La Concordia ★★★

44600 Alcañiz (Teruel)
Castillo de los Calatravos
Tel. (9)78-83 04 00 – Fax (9)78-83 03 66
Sr Cruz Sanchez

Rooms 12 with air-conditioning, telephone, bath, WC, TV and minibar; elevator. **Price** Double 14,500-12,500Pts. **Meals** Breakfast 1,100Pts, served 8:30-11:00, half board + 3,200Pts, +6,375Pts (per pers., 2 days min.). **Restaurant** Service 13:00-16:30, 20:30-23:00, menu 3,200Pts, also à la carte. Specialties: Ternasco asado - Costilletas a la baturra - Dulces tipicos. **Credit cards** All major. **Pets** Dogs not allowed. **Facilities** Parking. **Nearby** in Alcañiz: Colegiata Church - Calaceite (Plaza Mayor) - Gretas - Valderrobres - Monastery of Rueda in Escatrón - Morella - Ares del Maestre. **Open** 1. Feb - 11. Dec.

At the summit of a hill dominating Alcañiz, the present chateau dates mainly from the 18th century and was converted into a parador in 1968. Today it is the ideal setting for a romantic stay and everything helps make this hotel such a charming place. The decor is sober but in good taste: white walls, Spanish furniture and polished floors. The rooms on the courtyard are rather small and a bit sober: those looking over the town and the River Guadalupe are much lighter. The bathrooms are spacious and attractive. The menu allows one to appreciate specialties of Aragonese cuisine, and certainly do not leave without trying the Almendrades (confectionery of almond paste), a specialty of Alcañiz.

How to get there (Map 14): 103km southeast of Zaragoza via N232.

Hotel Monasterio de Piedra ★★★

50210 Nuévalos (Zaragoza)
Tel. (9)76-84 90 11 – Fax (9)76-84 90 54
Sr Montaner

Rooms 61 with telephone, bath, WC and TV. **Price** Single 7,000Pts, double 9,500Pts. **Meals** Breakfast 500Pts, served 8:00-10.30, half board + 3,100Pts, full board + 5,250Pts (per pers., 2 days min.). **Restaurant** Service 13:00-17:00, 21:00-23:00; menu 2,600Pts, also à la carte. Specialties: Migas - Trucha del monasterio - Ternasco de Aragòn. **Credit cards** All major. **Pets** Dogs allowed in the rooms. **Nearby** Alhama de Aragon - Jaraba - Cetina - Ariza - Catalayud. **Open** All year.

Founded in the 12th century by Cistercian monks, this remarkable well-conserved monastery has a great beauty. This is an astonishing site and a real and fresh oasis, full of greenery and rising right out of the Meseta, a dry and rugged region surrounded by steep sierras. Here the genius of man has associated with the genius of nature. One should for example note the monumental staircase, illuminated by opaque alabaster windows to give a dream-like light. The rooms are simple in the former monks' cells, with access via long and vaulted galleries. Some have terraces, others are located around the cloisters, yet others surround the entrance courtyard with its elm tree planted in 1681. Certainly do not leave the hotel without having visited the other parts of the monastery, and having walked in the woods with the many lakes, waterfalls and caves.

How to get there *(Map 14): 30km southwest of Catalayud via C202 to Nuévalos, then follow the signs for Monasterio de Piedra.*

Parador Fernando de Aragón ★★★

50680 Sos del Rey Católico (Zaragoza)
Arquitecto Sainz de Vicuña, 1
Tel. (9)48-88 80 11 - Fax (9)48-88 81 00
Sr Rizos Garrido

Rooms 65 with air-conditioning, telephone, bath, WC, TV and minibar; elevator. **Price** Double 10,500-12,500Pts. **Meals** Breakfast 1,200Pts, served 8:00-11:00, half board + 4,300Pts, full board + 6,375Pts. **Restaurant** Service 13:00-15:30, 20:30-22:30, menu 3,200Pts, also à la carte. Specialties: regional cooking. **Credit cards** All major. **Pets** Dogs not allowed. **Facilities** Parking. **Nearby** in Sos: San Esteban church - Uncastillo (Santa Maria Church and the Casa Consistorial). **Open** 25. Jan - 1. Dec.

Situated in the historically classified village of Sos, the Parador Fernando de Aragón was built a few years ago by one of the best Spanish architects, with respect for just one rule: the Aragonese style. Thus the craftsman's finish has been conserved and the stone already seems to have several centuries behind it. The rooms are very large with polished floor-tiles and beds of copper. Those on the second floor have a gallery, while the rooms on the third have balconies. The bathrooms are successfully realized and not short of practical fittings. The dining room on the fourth floor, with its massive pillars, overlooks the valley, and the restaurant is one of the best tables of the region.

How to get there (Map 6): 63km southeast of Pamplona via N240 towards Jaca, then C127.

Gran Hotel ★★★★

50001 Zaragoza
Calle Joaquin Costa, 5
Tel. (9)76-22 19 01 - Fax (9)76-23 67 13
Sra G. Elizaga

Rooms 140 with air-conditioning, telephone, bath, WC, cable TV and minibar; elevator. **Price** Single 12,000-13,700Pts, double 16,900Pts, suite 25,000-27,000Pts. **Meals** Breakfast 1,350Pts served 7:00-11:00. **Restaurant** Service 13:00-15:30, 20:00-23:00; menu 3,000Pts, also à la carte. Specialties: Meats. **Credit cards** All major. **Pets** Dogs allowed. **Facilities** Parking (1,700Pts). **Nearby** in Zaragoza: Basilica de Nuestra Señora del Pilar, La Seo, Palacio de la Aljaferta - Churches in Utebo, Alagon, San Mateo de Gàllego, Zuera - Cartuja Aula Dei - Pina. **Open** All year.

Opened in 1929 by King Alfonso XIII and recently restored, this hotel has known how to keep its class, and a delightful atmosphere and refinement, in a town where any establishment of character is sadly rare. The rather luxurious ambiance is not at all starchy. The large round lounge with its glazed roof is a good example of the elegant decor. The bedrooms are spacious and very comfortable, and decorated with taste, each with its own functional and very neat bathroom. For preference you can take the suite in which King Juan Carlos lived when a student at the Zaragoza military academy. A good welcome, an excellent quality-price ratio, and private parking are further reasons for choosing this hotel sited right in the town center.

How to get there (Map 15): near the Plaza del Dragón.

Hotel La Casona de Amandi ★★★

Amandi
33311 Villaviciosa (Asturias)
Tel. (9)8-589 01 30 - Fax (9)8-589 01 29
Sr R. Fernandez

Rooms 9 with telephone, bath, WC and TV. **Price** Double 10,500-13,900Pts.
Meals Breakfast 750Pts, served 8:30-10:30. **No Restaurant.Credit cards** All
major. **Pets** Dogs not allowed. **Facilities** Parking. **Nearby** In Amandi: Church of
San Juan; Fiesta de la Virgen del Protal (September) - Oviedo - Tazones - Roman
church of Priesca - Villabona - Monastery San Salvador of Valdedios. **Open** All
year, except in Jan.

Very well situated between sea and mountains, the little
village of Amandi is a real refuge of tranquility at the foot of
the first peaks of the Asturias, and yet only 15 kilometers from
the beaches. The 'casa' is a marvellous little house from the 19th
century that has kept all the atmosphere of a private house,
surrounded by a vast very green and flowery garden. The
beautiful rustic wooden planking has been retained, thick slats of
wood in the very large bedrooms, and all personalized with
antique furniture. In the very well equiped bathrooms the
original ceramics have been restored. Various small lounges
allow one to read, just rest or have breakfast provided one does
not prefer the winter garden arranged on the first floor. In the
fine weather one can then appreciate the large garden planted
with magnolias and other handsome trees. All the comforts and
good taste are to be found here, to ensure a most enjoyable stay.

How to get there (Map 3): 42 km northest of Oviedo.

Hotel La Arquera ★★★

La Arquera
33500 Llanes (Asturias)
Tel. (9)8-540 24 24 - Fax (9)8-540 01 75

Rooms 12 with telephone, bath, WC, TV,minibar and kitchen. **Price** 2 pers. 6,900Pts, 3 pers. 8,100-9,000Pts, 4 pers. 10,000/15,000Pts. **Meals** Breakfast 800Pts, served 8:30-10:00. **No restaurant. Credit cards** All major. **Pets** Dogs not allowed. **Facilities** Parking. **Nearby** Vidiago - Cave of Pindal in Pimiango - Beaches of Celorio and Nueva. **Open** All year.

At the foot of the Sierra de Cuera, Llanes is an attractive little port with a very picturesque old town quarter. Numerous beaches such as the 'Playa de Toro' and 'Playa del Sablon' have made its tourist reputation. The Spanish also come here to celebrate the local feasts, giving the 'Llaniscos' every occasion to remember all their traditions in a colorful manner. The hotel occupies a country house typical of this region, and has retained its grain store. At 2 kilometers from the village the hotel is well protected by its little garden. The glazed lounges have a wonderful view onto the mountains, while the bedrooms are large and well equiped for long stays, since as well as the traditional comforts, they also have small kitchens fitted with cookers, fridges, etc. Some rooms cater for up to four people. Besides the pleasures of the beach—do not miss those of the small village of Celorio and ay Nueva, the 'Playa del Mar'—the region is rich in prehistoric sites that are all of interest.

How to get there (Map 15): 96km west of Santander, and 2km south of Llanes.

La Posada de Babel ★★★

La Pereda
33509 Llanes (Asturias)
Tel. (9)8-540 25 25 - Fax (9)8-540 25 25

Rooms 8 with air-conditioning, telephone, bath, WC and TV. **Price** Double 8,100-10,500Pts. **Meals** Breakfast 850Pts, served 8:00-10:30. **Restaurant** Service 13:00-15:00, 20:30-22:00; closed Tues and Feb; carte 3,000-4,500Pts. Specialties: regional cooking. **Credit cards** Visa, Eurocard, MasterCard. **Pets** Dogs not allowed. **Facilities** Bikes, practise golf, parking. **Nearby** Vidiago - Cave of Pindal in Pimiango - Beaches of Celorio and Nueva. **Open** All year.

In this beautiful region of the Asturias, La Posada de Babel offers a quality retreat for those appreciating the serenity of an all calming nature, but also with the possibility–less than 3 kilometers away–of plunging into the more lively ambiance of the beaches. The hotel enjoys a superb site looking over fields and woods, surrounded by a park of more than 1 hectare, planted with magnolias, apple trees and camelias. The house is a beautiful modern construction in the spirit of Le Corbusier. The ground floor shelters the lounge, library and dining room, and via a large glazed gallery directly communes with nature. The more traditional interior has kept a very warm ambiance: classical furniture in good taste, beautiful canvasses and lithographs on the walls and an open fire in season. The same cosy atmosphere is in the bedrooms, and five of them have terraces. Our preference is for No. 8, a tiny little house on two floors in the garden, but always with the same charming decoration, both simple but carefully chosen. The restaurant is excellent and along with the daily market, it lets you try the specialties of the region. To better appreciate the surroundings, the hotel has bikes available and can also organize horse riding, or 4x4 outings.

How to get there (Map 4): 96 km from Santander, and 4 km south of Llanes.

Hotel de la Reconquista ★★★★★

33004 Oviedo (Asturias)
Calle Gil de Jaz, 16
Tel. (9)8-524 11 00 - Fax (9)8-524 11 66
Sr Cantin

Rooms 142 with air-conditioning, telephone, bath, WC, TV and minibar; elevator. **Price** Single 17,300-21,600Pts, Double 21,600-27,000Pts, suite 32,000-64,000Pts. **Meals** Breakfast 1,800Pts, served 7:00-10:30; half board + 6,000Pts, full board + 10,000Pts (per pers.). **Restaurant** Service 13:30-16:00, 21:00-23:30; menu 5,000Pts, also à la carte. Specialty: Fabada .**Credit cards** All major. **Pets** Dogs not allowed. **Facilities** Sauna (1,200Pts), garage. **Nearby** Uncastillo (Churc of Santa Maria and Casa Consistorial) - Road of Longas. **Open** All year.

This former hospice-hospital was built in the 18th century by the renowned architect P. A. Menendez. The building has only two floors but is dominated by a huge Spanish coat of arms in the center, a remarkable example of baroque sculpture. Having traversed the porch, you find yourself in a vast rectangular lounge lit by a glazed roof. A mezzanine runs all around and is supported by a double stone colonnade. The hotel offers exceptional facilities: a gym, a sauna, conference rooms, and also a concert hall set out in the very beautiful chapel, with an octagonal plan and two tiers of superposed seating. The bedrooms and service are those of a real palace.

How to get there (Map 3): in the town center near the San Francisco Park.

La Rectoral ★★★★

33775 Taramundi-La Villa (Asturias)
Tél. (9)8 564 67 67 - Fax (9)8 564 67 77
Sr Barrenechea

Rooms 18 with air-conditioning, telephone, bath, WC, cable TV and minibar; elevator. **Price** Single 10,000-12,000Pts, double 12,000-15,000Pts, 3 pers. 15,000-18,000Pts. **Meals** Breakfast 950Pts, served 7:00-11:00; half board 16,500Pts (per pers.). **Restaurant** Service 13:00-15:00, 21:00-22:00; menu 2,200Pts. **Credit cards** All major. **Pets** Dogs not allowed. **Facilities** Sauna, garage. **Nearby** Mazo de Meredo - Tapia de Casariego - Castropol - Figueras. **Open** All year.

This is one of the most charming of Spanish inns, in the heart of deepest Spain in a tiny village on the frontier between the Asturias and Galicia–and so the local reputation is based not on its cutlery alone! This former 18th-century presbytery has been transformed into a comfortable hotel. The barn has become the lounge, and next to it a bar (where the barman will introduce you to the local liqueur, pacharan), and then the dining room. The bedrooms have been decorated in the traditional style of the Asturias, and are welcoming, opening onto a small private terrace with a superb view over the gentle green hills. Everything here is simple, very authentic and top quality. A good halting place for discovering a different Spain.

How to get there *(Map 2): 65km northeast of Lugo, via N640 to Vilaodriz; then take the small road on the right.*

Palacete Peñalba ★★★

42100 Figueras del Mar (Asturias)
El Cotalero
Tel. (9)8-563 61 25

Rooms 18 with telephone, bath or shower, WC and TV. **Price** Single 7,000Pts, double 9,700Pts, suite 12,000Pts. **Meals** Breakfast 600Pts, served at any time. **Restaurant** "Peñalba", av. Trenor-Puerto, service 13:00-15:00, 20:00-22:00; carte 4,200-5,800Pts. Specialty: fish. **Credit cards** Amex, Visa, Eurocard, MasterCard. **Pets** Small dogs allowed. **Facilities** Parking. **Nearby** Beaches - Valley of Masma via N634 from Barreiros (Lourenza, Lindin). **Open** All year.

Built in 1912 by a disciple of Gaudi, the Palacete Peñalba is about to be classified a historic monument. Converted into a hotel five years ago, it has a rather faded charm, an impression given off by the colors and furnishings, but not at all by the irreproachable amenities and comfort. The bedrooms will delight any lover of big spaces, while Numbers 12, 14 and 15 have large terraces. In the suites the bathrooms are set in a veranda. Very peaceful, the house is surrounded by a garden planted with various species of pine trees, along with a superb palm tree. There is no restaurant in the hotel but at the little port of Figueras, just 200 meters away, the same proprietor also owns a restaurant whose renown has spread beyond the frontier of the Asturias and even of Spain, are in large part to the excellent fisch dishes.

How to get there (Map 2): 150km northeast of Oviedo, on the coast and 3km from Ribadeo.

Hotel Lopez de Haro ★★★★★

48009 Bilbao
Obispo Orueta, 2 et 4
Tel. (9)4-423 55 00 - Fax (9)4-423 45 00
M. Javier Muñoz

Rooms 53 with air-conditioning, telephone, bath, WC, TV and minibar; elevator. **Price** Single 15,280-16,755Pts, double 21,165Pts, suite 25,620-30,865Pts. **Meals** Breakfast 450Pts, served 7:00-11.00. **Restaurant** "Club Nautico" service 13:00-15:30, 20:00-23:30; closed Sat lunch, Sun and National Holidays; buffet (lunch): 3,500-4,000Pts, menus 5,300-6,300Pts, also à la carte. Specialties: Ensalada de bovabante, merluche mariscale. **Credit cards** All major. **Pets** Dogs not allowed. **Facilities** Sauna, garage. **Nearby** in Bilbao: Fine Art Museum - Nuestra Señora de Begoña - Campo de la Bilbaina golf course and Neguri golf course (18-Hole). **Open** All year.

This superb hotel occupies the former headquarters of the republican newspaper, "El Liberal", but behind the very classical and almost austere facade, a real jewel is hidden. The reception hall is particularly attractive with marble alongside green ivy, which makes for a remarkable effect. The caisson ceilings of the restaurant, the dainty tables with their pink linen and lamps, the elevator with its sparkling brass, or the very English bar with its soft club armchairs–all the details are carefully thought out. But however luxurious it may be, the hotel still keeps its warm character. In the bedrooms the walls have been left bare of any decoration and the effect is very successful: very comfortable, along with their very beautiful bathrooms. In the kitchens a French chef is in charge, and on the tables one finds Limoges porcelain and Bohemian crystal glassware. The welcome is always attentive and stylish, to crown the overall effect.

How to get there (Map 5): in the town center.

Hotel San Roman de Escalante ★★★★

39795 Escalante (Cantabria)
Carretera de Escalante a Castillo, Km 2
Tel. (9)4-267 77 45 – Fax (9)4-267 76 43
Sr Melis

Rooms 9 with air-conditioning, telephone, bath, WC, TV and minibar. **Price** Double 13,000-25,000Pts. **Meals** Breakfast 975Pts, served 8:00-10:30; half board + 4,725Pts, full board + 8,250Pts (per pers.). **Restaurant** Service 13:30-16:00, 21:00-23:30; menu 5,000Pts, also à la carte. Specialty: Fabada. **Credit cards** All major. **Pets** Dogs allowed. **Facilities** Parking. **Nearby** à Santoña: Church of Santa Maria and Monastery of Montehano - Noja - Romanesque church of Bareyo - Beaches of Isla and Ajo. **Open** 18. Jan - 18. Dec.

Escalante is a few kilometers away from the important fishing port of Santoña whose fortress has defended the deep bay cutting into the land since the 17th-century. The hotel owes its name to the hermitage dating from Roman times and on the property. The house is a former noble residence whose fine walls rise out of a garden shaded by trees, and in which sculptures by contemporary artists are on display. Here one actually lives surrounded by works of art, both old and modern, as the hotel also has an art gallery and boutique selling antiques. The former stables have been converted into a very good gastronomic restaurant which contributes to the reputation. Comfort is excellent in the rooms which are large with their little lounge areas. This is a very good address from which to discover – in luxury – the Cantabrian coastland.

How to get there *(Map 4): 42km east of Santander*

La Tahona de Besnes

33578 Alles (Cantabria)
Tél. (9)8 541 42 49 / 8 541 57 49 – Fax (9)8 541 44 72

Rooms 25 with telephone, bath, WC and TV. **Price** Single 4,575-6,335Pts, double 5,720-7,920Pts, 4 pers. 10,000-14,000Pts. **Meals** Breakfast 750Pts, served 8:00-10.30; half board + 2,450Pts, full board 4,100Pts. **Restaurant** Service 13:00-15:30, 20:30-23:00; menu 1,750Pts. Specialties: regional cooking. **Credit cards** Visa, Eurocard, MasterCard. **Pets** Dogs not allowed. **Facilities** Parking. **Nearby** Covadonga National Park - The Cares Route (C632) between Cangas de Onis and Panes - Walks in the Cares Gorges. **Open** All year.

Between Oviedo and Santander stretches the mountain chain of the 'Picos de Europa' (the Peaks of Europe), that offers magnificent attractions to all nature lovers: trails, gorges and rivers filled with salmon and trout. This site has favored rural tourism such as one finds it at Allès. Access to the little village is through of a forest with many winding little streams. Several former farm buildings shelter the rooms, and the decor is very rustic, very sober and very authentic-but one finds all the comforts of a traditional hotel, although you should note that all bathrooms only have small hip-baths. All is calm and one rediscovers the scents of the countryside-and with the cock's crow for alarm clock ! A young and enthusiastic team runs the house and they suggest all kinds of activities: bike rental, canoe outings through the gorges of the Cares and the Deva, 4x4 excursions, horse riding-and more. If you add the sea, some thirty kilometers away, to the program one has everything for a very good holiday.

How to get there *(Map 4): 89km west of Santander to Panes and Alles. Then, take road to Cangas de Onis for 10,5km.*

Hotel Hosteria de Quijas ★★★

39590 Quijas (Cantabria)
Carret. N 634
Tel. (9)42-82 08 33 - Fax (9)42-83 80 50
Sr Castaneda

Rooms 14 and 5 suites with telephone, bath, WC, cable TV and minibar; elevator. **Price** Single 8,500Pts, Double 10,000Pts, suite 17,000Pts. **Meals** Breakfast 600Pts, served 7:00-11:00. **Restaurant** Service 13:30-15:30, 20:30-23:00; closed Sun from Nov to Jan; carte. Specialties: Ensalada templada de mollejas de pato y habitas - Calabacines rellenos de bacalaò tres salsas. **Credit cards** All major. **Pets** Dogs not allowed. **Facilities** Swimming pool, parking. **Nearby** Santander - Altamira Caves; Pedreña golf course (18-Hole). **Open** 4. Jan - 20. Dec.

A longing for peace and quiet? Then go and hide in the Hotel Hosteria de Quijas, this former 18th-century palace set in a magnificent garden with its centuries-old trees and superb magnolias. The bedrooms are refined and furnished only with pieces from the 17th and 18th centuries. Small lounges are scattered through the hotel. Uncovered stonework, caisson ceilings and the 'Thonet style' all contribute to its charm. The dining room is welcoming with its wooden beams and pillars. A variety of trips can be planned starting from this site, so why not try a little new country?

How to get there *(Map 4): 25km southeast of Santander to Torrelavega, towards Oviedo, Puente San Miguel and Quijas.*

Hotel Real ★★★★★

39005 Santander (Cantabria)
El Sardinero – Paseo Pérez Galdós, 28
Tel. (9)42-27 25 50 – Fax (9)42-27 45 73
Sr Armengol

Rooms 123 with air-conditioning, telephone, bath, WC, cable TV and minibar; elevator. **Price** Single 15,850-28,800Pts, Double 19,800-36,000Pts, suite 40,000-130,000Pts. **Meals** Breakfast 1,400Pts, served 7:00-11:00. **Restaurant** Service 13:30-15:30, 21:00-23:30; menu 3,200Pts, also à la carte. Specialties: regional and international cooking. **Credit cards** All major. **Pets** Dogs not allowed. **Facilities** Parking. **Nearby** Santander - Altamira Caves; Pedreña golf course (18-Hole). **Open** All year.

This hotel, a racecourse and casino were built in Santander when the royal family used to have its summer quarters in this town, and one sought to give the town those facilities to satisfy all the requirement of such visitors. No details were spared and the hotel was given a privileged site overlooking the Bay of Santander and the Magdalena Beach. Since then it has of course been transformed and renovated, but it has retained all the magnificence and luxury of an old and rather dated hotel 'de luxe'. All the bedrooms open onto terraces or balconies, which are often flowered. The atmosphere here is one of calm and the furniture is classical Empire style. One 'plus' is the dining room with its veranda and stone arcades, and carefully selected furnishings. Next door are cosy lounges. All this to constitute a luxurious staging post in Cantabria.

How to get there (Map 4): 3.5km northeast of Santander (El Sardinero).

66

Parador Gil Blas ★★★

39330 Santillana del Mar (Cantabria)
Plaza Ramón Pelayo, 11
Tel. (9)42-81 80 00 - Fax (9)42-81 83 91
Sr Garralda Iribarren

Rooms 56 with telephone, bath, WC, TV and minibar; elevator. **Price** Double 16,500Pts. **Meals** Breakfast 1,200Pts, served 8:00-11:00; full board + 6,375Pts (per pers., 3 days min.) **Restaurant** Service 13:00-16:00, 20:30-22:30; menu 3,200Pts, also à la carte. Specialties: Cocido - Merluza - Lubina - Salmón - Ternera al queso. **Credit cards** All major. **Pets** Dogs not allowed. **Facilities** Sauna, garage, parking. **Nearby** Colegiata de Santillana del Mar - Altamira Caves - Comillas - Picos de Europa - Beaches of Cobreces and Suances. **Open** All year.

Situated on the village square, the hotel occupies the very old and imposing home of the Barreda-Bracho family. The interior architecture is typical of the region: simple wooden columns give structure to most rooms, while the floors are shingled or of polished large parquet chips. On each floor there is a large lounge by the corridor leading to the rooms, which are very attractive: beds with columns in the Spanish style and everywhere a very beautiful choice of furniture, various objects and pictures. However, a special mention must be made of room 222 with its panoramic terrace over the village roofs and countryside. You will thus appreciate the calm in this region, while the caves of Altamira attract a large number of visitors.

How to get there (Map 4): 31km southwest of Santander via N634, then C6316.

Hotel Altamira ★★★

39330 Santillana del Mar (Cantabria)
Calle Canton, 1
Tel. (9)42-81 80 25 - Fax (9)42-81 80 25
Sr Oceja Bujan

Rooms 32 with telephone, shower, WC and cable TV. **Price** Single 5,000-8,250Pts, double 9,900-10,850Pts. **Meals** Breakfast 600Pts, served 8:00-11:00; full board 8,375Pts (per pers.) **Restaurant** with air-conditioning, service 13:15-16:00, 20:00-22:45; menu 1,650Pts, also à la carte. Specialties: Cocido montañes - Ensalada cantabra de salmon y almejas - Solomillo al vino tinto de rioja. **Credit cards** All major. **Pets** Dogs not allowed. **Nearby** Colegiata de Santillana del Mar - Altamira Caves - Comillas - Picos de Europa - Beaches of Cobreces and Suances. **Open** All year.

The Hotel Altamira now occupies one of the aristocratic houses of Santillana, a medieval town classified as a historic monument, that has conserved a beautiful collection of residences and palaces. Many still wear the shields and arms of the knights and hidalgos who lived in them. This palace of the Valdevesco, rebuilt at the start of the 19th century, is a simple hotel but in goodtaste. The decor is sober and rustic in the lounges and two restaurants, with one of them serving only regional specialties. Beside the staircases and on the half-landings, one finds small corners for reading, TV rooms and other amenities. The bedrooms offer good comfort but those on the upper floor are smaller and only have showers. To be noted: a delightful terrace and a nice place to enjoy a drink.

How to get there *(Map 4): 31km southwest of Santander via N634, then C6316.*

Hotel Los Infantes ★★★

39330 Santillana del Mar (Cantabria)
Avenida le Dorat, 1
Tel. (9)42-81 81 00 - Fax (9)42-84 01 03
Sr G. Mesones

Rooms 30 with telephone, bath and WC. **Price** Single 4,000-10,000Pts, double 6,000-14,000Pts. **Meals** Breakfast 600Pts, served 8:00-11:00; half board 5,600-9,600Pts, full board 6,900-10,900Pts (per pers.) **Restaurant** Service 13:00-16:00, 20:00-23:00; menu 2,000Pts, also à la carte. Specialties: Cocido montañes - Quesada en lechefritas - Solomillo al queso. **Credit cards** All major. **Pets** Dogs allowed in the rooms. **Nearby** Colegiata de Santillana del Mar - Altamira Caves - Comillas - Picos de Europa - Beaches of Cobreces and Suances. **Open** All year.

The Hotel Los Infantes now occupies the ancient house of the Calderon and its facade still bears their shield and arms. Right from the entrance one notices the intimate atmosphere that reigns in the hotel, where everything has been designed so that the traveller should feel a little bit at home. On the ground floor one finds a welcoming reception area and dining room with an open fireplace. Upstairs there is a beautiful lounge. One finds the same spirit in the bedrooms, but our favorites are those on the main front facade, which are more spacious, and two of them also have small lounges. Good regional cuisine, a cordial welcome and a discotheque are found here, but the latter does not annoy those staying.

How to get there (Map 4): *31km southwest of Santander via N634, then C6316.*

Hotel Don Pablo ★★

39710 Solares (Cantabria)
General Mola,6
Tél. (9)42 52 21 20 - Fax (9)42 52 05 26
M. Oceja Mazas

Rooms 27 with air-conditioning, telephone, bath, WC and cable TV. **Price** Single 5,000-8,000Pts, Double 8,000-10,000Pts. **Meals** Breakfast 450Pts, served 8:00-11:00; half board + 5,000Pts, full board + 6000Pts. **Restaurant** Service 13:00-16:00, 20:00-24:00; carte 3,300-4,000Pts. Specialties: regional cooking. **Credit cards** All major. **Pets** Dogs not allowed. **Facilities** Garage, parking. **Nearby** Santander - Palacio de Acevedo in Hoznayo - Palacio de L'Eseldo in Pàmanes - Casa de Cantolla and Palacio de Rañada in Liérganes - Puento Viergos Caves. **Open** All year.

In the back-country behind the Cantabrian coast, Solares is a thermal spa known for its mineral waters, but the village and hotel are only really interesting because they are some twenty kilometers away from all the bustle of Santander. The building is an aristocratic house from the 16th century, and has retained its superb coat of arms and beautiful chapel. All the rest has been converted in the traditional, even standard manner: a rustic atmosphere with stylish furniture, beams and terra-cotta tiled flooring. Comfort is fully assured with one or two extra services such as an internal video channel and satellite TV. Only a few rooms but no less than three restaurants, so one can understand that the hotel hosts a lot of receptions. An agreeable staging post rather than a place to stay.

How to get there (Map 4): 16km east of Santander.

Hotel Pikes ★★★★★

07800 Ibiza
San Antonio de Portmany
Tel. (9)71 34 22 22 - Fax (9)71 34 23 12
Sr A. Pikes

Rooms 24 with air-conditioning, telephone, bath, WC, TV and minibar. **Price** Single 16,300-20,000Pts, double 18,000-25,000Pts, suite 30,000-55,000Pts, duplex 60,000-90,000Pts. **Meals** Breakfast included, served 8.30-12.00; half board + 2,150Pts (per pers.). **Restaurant** Service 13:00-15:30, 20:30-24:00; carte. Specialties: international and regional cooking. **Credit cards** All major. **Pets** Dogs allowed. **Facilities** Swimming pool, parking. **Nearby** Dalt Vila and the cathedral of Ibiza - Beach of Talamanca; Roca Llisa golf course (9-Hole) **Open** 1. Mar - 31. Jan.

To uncover a hotel hidden away between gardens and pine woods on Ibiza is something of a record! This is, however, the case with the Hotel Pikes, a residence ahat is 600 years old. With only twenty rooms all differently decorated, but in the typical style of the island, the Hotel Pikes offers all the advantages of a hotel 'de luxe' along with the informal ambiance of a friend's home. Not very far from the nightlife, you can rest and recover here during the afternoon beside the swimming pool after a heavy night out! With a bit of luck, you may also spot Julio (Iglesias) or possibly Grace (Jones). All things said, this is a tiny paradise.

How to get there *(Map 9): by boat from Barcelona and Valencia: contact the Cia. Transmediterránea company (Tel. (971) 72 67 40).*

Les Terrasses

07800 Ibiza
Carret. de Santa Eulalia, km 1
Tel. (9)71-33 26 43 - Fax (9)71-33 11 61
Sra Pialoux

Rooms 9 with heating or air-conditioning, telephone, bath and WC. **Price** Single 12,500-14,500Pts, double 14,500-18,000Pts. **Meals** Breakfast included, served 8:30-10.00. **Restaurant** Open Tuesday and Wednesday; menu 4,300Pts, also à la carte. Specialty: Fish. **Credit cards** Visa, Eurocard, MasterCard. **Pets** Dogs allowed. **Facilities** Swimming pool, tennis, parking. **Nearby** Dalt Vila and the cathedral of Ibiza - Beach of Talamanca; Roca Llisa golf course (9-Hole). **Open** All year.

Les Terrasses has nothing to with a hotel—one comes here as a friend! A confidential location, only a large indigo blue stone at 1km on the road from Santa Eulalia indicates the entrance. Françoise, your host, is French and has converted this old house of the Ibizan countryside with a lot of talent. The washed ocres and indigos, the white chalked walls set off with blue door and window frames—all give the house a truly authentic character. There is the same charm indoors where the antique furniture, carefully selected at the local 'flea markets', is mingled with the family pieces. The bedrooms have this same simplicity and good taste. The cuisine is good: light and fresh at lunch-time, but more prepared dishes at dinner. One can be deliciously idle by the swimming pool or on the beautiful shaded terrace, where a delightful time may be had despite its location on a touristy island. This is a very agreeable place to stay.

How to get there (Map 9): from Barcelona and Valencia: contact the Cia. Transmediterránea company (Tel. (971) 72 67 40); on the road towards Santa Eulalia, a blue stone on the right indicates the way.

El Corsario

07800 Ibiza
Poniente 5 Dalt Vila
Tel. (9)71-30 12 48 - Fax (9)71-39 19 53

Rooms 14 with telephone and shower. **Price** Single 3,500-6,000Pts, double 6,000-12,000Pts, suite 16,000-20,000Pts. **Meals** Breakfast included, served 8:30-10.00. **Restaurant** By reservation, service 21:00-22:30; menus 2,200-4,200Pts. **Credit cards** Visa, Eurocard, MasterCard. **Pets** Dogs not allowed. **Nearby** Dalt Vila and the cathedral of Ibiza - Beach of Talamanca; Roca Llisa golf course (9-Hole) **Open** All year.

An agreeable small hotel hidden in the old town, El Corsario is one of the oldest hotels on Ibiza, and the simplicity of this old house is one of its major charms. The hotel is very well kept and the service friendly; breakfast may be taken on the terrace. This abounds with pots of flowers, and from it you have one of the best views of Ibiza. One can dine at the hotel but a reservation is needed; prices are very modest compared to others on this island.

How to get there *(Map 9): by boat from Barcelona and Valencia: contact the Cia. Transmediterránea company (Tel. (971) 72 67 40); in the old town (Dalt Vila).*

Ca's Pla

07800 Ibiza
San Miguel de Balanzat - P.O.Box N° 777
Tel. (9)71-33 45 87 - Fax (9)71-33 46 04
Sr N. Sanchez de Fenaroli

Rooms 14 with telephone, bath, WC and TV. **Price** Single 12,000-16,000Pts, double 18,000-20,000Pts, suite 20,000-25,000Pts. **Meals** Breakfast included, served 8:00-10:00. **Restaurant** Reservation for dinner; lunch at the swimming pool. Specialties: Fish, barbecue, paella. **Credit cards** Visa, Eurocard, MasterCard. **Pets** Dogs not allowed. **Facilities** Swimming pool, tennis (800Pts), parking. **Nearby** Dalt Vila and the cathedral of Ibiza - Beach of Talamanca; Roca Llisa golf course (9-Hole). **Open** 1. Apr - 30. Nov.

In the northwest of the island and some twenty kilometers from Ibiza and close to the port of San Miguel, the owners of this large villa have opened 14 rooms for their guests. You are here in a holiday home, received as friends, which means that you will be living in a very personalized and very warm atmosphere: lots of objects, souvenirs, books, bouquets of dried flowers and so on. All the public rooms open wide onto the garden alive with plants and flowers, while the shady terrace offers many small and restful corners, and hammocks and armchairs allow one to be comfortably idle. The rooms have all been decorated with a care for decor, comfort and your well-being. You are asked not to just drop by on the off-chance, but to book well in advance so that "the bees can get to work" to better receive you.

How to get there *(Map 9): by plane: from Barcelona, Madrid, Alicante, Valencia to Ibiza; by ferry: from Barcelona, Valencia to Ibiza. To the northwest of Ibiza, at San Miguel take the road for the port. At 14km take the roadon your right.*

La Residencia ★★★★

Mallorca 07179 Deia (Mallorca)
Finca Son Canals
Tel. (9)71-63 90 11 - Fax (9)71-63 93 70
Sra Cariuu

Rooms 27 with air-conditioning, telephone, bath, WC, cable TV and minibar.
Price Double 20,750-28,000Pts, suite 26,500-36,500Pts. **Meals** Breakfast
included, served 8:00-11:30. **Restaurant** Service 12:30-15:00, 20:00-23:00;
carte 4,400-7,150Pts. **Credit cards** All major. **Pets** Dogs not allowed.
Facilities Swimming pool, tennis, parking. **Nearby** Palma - Northroad
(Miramar, San Marroig, Lluc Alcari, Cala) - Monastery Real Cartuja de
Valdemossa; Son Vida golf course (18-Hole). **Open** All year.

A real love affair with La Residencia hotel ! Fifteen
kilometers from Majorca and far from the tourist traps, lies
hidden a village full of charm, a small casket with a real jewel at
its heart. A 16th-century manor house converted into a
hotel—and today one of the most delightful in the whole of
Spain. One discovers hectares of woodlands, terraces with
flowers sprouting out of the old stonework, flowered balconies
and a succession of patios around the hotel. With its swimming
pool facing the mountains, La Residencia is a genuine oasis.
The owner is a great collector of pictures which cover all the
walls. The bedrooms are vast and well furnished, all with great
refinement. La Residencia is without doubt one of our favorite
hotels for reconciling you and the Balearics, all too often
stripped of all charm by the affluence of tourists.

*How to get there (Map 9): by boat from Barcelona and Valencia: contact the
Cia. Transmediterránea company (Tel. (971) 72 67 40); 27km north of Palma.*

Grand Hotel Palacio Valderràbanos ★★★★

05001 Avila
Plaza de la Catédral, 9
Tel. (9)20-21 10 23 - Fax (9)20-25 16 91
Sr Beltrán - Sr J.-M. Caz

Rooms 73 with air-conditioning, telephone, bath, WC, cable TV, safe and minibar; elevator. **Price** Single 9,000Pts, double 14,000Pts. **Meals** Breakfast included (buffet), served 8:00-11.00; half board + 4,700Pts, full board + 8,400Pts (per pers., 2 days min.). **Restaurant** Service 13:00-15:30, 20:00-23:00; menu 3,700Pts, also à la carte. **Credit cards** All major. **Pets** Dogs allowed in the rooms. **Nearby** in Avila: Cathedral, Murallas (walls), Basilica de San Vicente, Monastery of Santo Tòmas - Cebreros. **Open** All year.

The Palacio Valderràbanos is near the cathedral in the very beautiful town of Avila, snug within its impressive walls dating from the 11th century, and with ramparts and 88 towers still surrounding half the town. The hotel's austere facade sets off the granite entry arch from the 16th century, which still bears the shield and arms of the two noble families that used to live here. Inside reigns a calm ambiance and all the rooms are comfortable, but we still recommend the suite and duplex set in the tower itself, or again, room number 126 with its balcony giving onto the cathedral. The welcome is always excellent.

How to get there *(Map 12): 97km southeast of Salamanca via N501: or 111km northwest of Madrid via A6, exit Villacastín, then N110.*

Parador Raimundo de Borgoña ★★★

05001 Avila
Marqués de Canales de Chozas, 16
Tel. (9)20-21 13 40 - Fax (9)20-22 61 66
Sr della Torre Alcala

Rooms 62 with air-conditioning, telephone, bath, WC, TV and minibar. **Price** Double 11,000-12,000Pts. **Meals** Breakfast 1,200Pts, served 8:00-11:00. **Restaurant** Service 13:00-16:00, 20:30-23:00; menu 3,200Pts, also à la carte. Specialties: Judias del barco - Cochinillo asado. **Credit cards** Visa, Eurocard, MasterCard. **Pets** Dogs not allowed. **Nearby** in Avila: Cathedral, Murallas (walls), Basilica de San Vicente, Monastery of Santo Tòmas - Cebreros. **Open** All year.

This Parador bears the name of the man who reconquered, repeopled and reconstructed Avila, also giving it the fantastic walls, which like an immense crown encircle the ancient 'Town of the Knights'. The hotel was built on the ruins of the Benavides palace and still conserves some of the original structure: one of its facades, backing onto the walls, forms one side of the square, which you enter via one of the nine town gates, La Puerta del Carmen. This ideal location is the main 'plus' of the hotel, apart from which the decor is all rather standardized. This said however, there are no complaints about the rooms and all are comfortable and well-equiped. One should certainly try for a room overlooking the square. Construction work is planned at the parador, so be sure to check about this.

How to get there (Map 12): 97km southeast of Salamanca via N501: or 111km northwest of Madrid via A6, exit Villacastín, then N110.

Hostería de Bracamonte ★★★

05001 Avila
C./ Bracamonte, 6
Tel. (9)20-25 12 80 / 21 28 66
Sr Costa

Rooms 16 with telephone, bath, WC and TV. **Price** Single 8,000-9,000Pts, double 15,000-17,000Pts. **Meals** Breakfast 400Pts, served 8:00-10:30; full board + 4,590Pts (per pers.). **Restaurant** Service 12:30-16:00, 20:00-24:00; menu 2,000Pts, also à la carte. Specialties: regional cooking. **Credit cards** All major. **Pets** Dogs allowed in the room. **Nearby** in Avila: Cathedral, Murallas (walls), Basilica de San Vicente, Monastery of San Tòmas - Cebreros. **Open** All year.

In the heart of Avila and two paces from the Plaza de la Victoria, a pretty little hotel has opened in which particular care has been given to the decor. The entry hall attracts with its plain stonework, discreet lighting, the magnificent tapestries on the walls and the bright tiles of the floor. Around are spread the different restaurant rooms, which one enters under some pretty vaulting. The bar is decorated with photos of personalities of Spanish life who have honored it with their presence, and it is a very lively spot. A stone staircase leads to the rooms furnished in an elegant Castillian style; one suite deserves special mention for its slightly mansarded ceiling, which is very delightful. In a town not famous for night-life, you will find a very attractive ambiance both in the restaurant and bar, before dropping peacefully off to sleep sheltered by such beautiful walls.

How to get there (Map 12): 97km southeast of Salamanca via N501: or 111km northwest of Madrid via A6, exit Villacastín, then N110.

Parador de Gredos ★★★

05132 Novarredonda (Avila)
Carretera Barraco, km 43 - Bejar
Tel. (9)20-34 80 48 - Fax (9)20-34 82 05
Sr Alonso Almeida

Rooms 77 with telephone, bath, WC, cable TV and minibar. **Price** Double 9,500-11,500Pts, suite 10,000-13,000Pts. **Meals** Breakfast 1,200Pts (buffet), served 8:00-10:30; half board + 4,200Pts, full board + 6,375Pts (per pers.). **Restaurant** Service 13:30-15:30, 20:30-23:00; menu 3,200Pts, also à la carte. Specialties: Castilian and international cooking. **Credit cards** All major. **Pets** Dogs not allowed. **Facilities** Tennis, riding, parking (1,000Pts). **Nearby** Sierra de Gredos - Puerto del Pico (1,352 m/4,435 ft) - Cuevas del Valle - Monbeltràn - Avila. **Open** All year.

Not far from Madrid rises the large hill called the 'Sierra de Gredos', and in 1926 King Alfonso XIII ordered that the first parador in Spain should be built on it. Hereabouts the winter is particularly severe, which is why the architecture relies on massive stonework, so attractive and giving a real impression of grandeur, notably to the columns and terraces. Inside, and as if to counter the cold, the lase of wood has been generous: it is everywhere and very attractive as well. The rooms are vast as in every parador, and furnished in the Castillian style. From the hotel one can enjoy all the pleasures of both hunting and fishing, while Avila is only 60 kilometers away and absolutely deserves a visit, as it is one of the most mythical and most attractive towns of Spain.

How to get there *(Map 12): 116km west of Madrid via A6, on the road linking Ávila to Talavera de la Reina.*

Landa Palace ★★★★★

09000 Burgos
km 236 Carret. Madrid Irun
Tel. (9)47-20 63 43 - Fax (9)47-26 46 76
Sr Revuelta

Rooms 37 and 5 suites with air-conditioning, telephone, bath, WC, TV, safe and minibar. **Price** Single 12,000-14,000Pts, double 16,000-32,000Pts, suite 35,000Pts. **Meals** Breakfast 1,500Pts, served 8:00-11:00. **Restaurant** Service 13:00-16:00, 21:00-23:30; menu 5,800Pts, also à la carte. Specialties: Fish. **Credit cards** Visa, Eurocard, MasterCard. **Pets** Dogs not allowed. **Facilities** Swimming pool, garage (1,200Pts). **Nearby** in Burgos: Cathedral - Monasterio de las Huelgas Reales (Royal Convent) - Cartuja de Miraflores (Gothic charterhouse) - Monasterio de San Salvador at Oña - Church Santa Maria la Real de Sasomòn. **Open** All year.

The owner of a restaurant in Madrid, Mr Landa bought an ancient 14th-century military tower some thirty years ago. He had it taken down and rebuilt stone by stone some twenty kilometers from its original site. Two wings were added and the hotel opened its doors in 1964. The Landa Palace is very beautiful, very luxurious, very refined, and shelters some charming collections as well: a collection of carriages in the courtyard, of watch movements on the ground floor, of pressing irons, tools, and weighing scales–among others. The service and fittings of the rooms are perfect, but if you really prefer the truly 'grande luxe', go for the royal suite. For more silence, opt for those rooms overlooking the countryside and swimming pool. The pool is 'Hollywoodian' and covered with a gothic vaulting roof.

How to get there (Map 4): 3km south of Burgos via N1.

Mesòn del Cid

09003 Burgos
Plaza Santa Maria, 8
Tel. (9)47-20 59 71 - Fax (9)47-26 94 60
Sr Lopez Alzaga

Rooms 28 with bath or shower, WC, and TV. **Price** Single 7,500Pts, double 13,000Pts, suite 18,000Pts. **Meals** Breakfast 900Pts, served 8:00-11:30. **Restaurant** Service 13:00-16:00, 20:00-24:00; menus 3,000-4,100Pts. Specialties: Alubias rojas - Cordero Lechal asado - Postre del abuelo. **Credit cards** Amex, Visa, Eurocard, MasterCard. **Pets** Dogs not allowed. **Facilities** Garage (1,000Pts). **Nearby** in Burgos: Cathedral - Monasterio de las Huelgas Reales (Royal Convent) - Cartuja de Miraflores (Gothic charterhouse) - Monasterio de San Salvador at Oña - Church Santa Maria la Real de Sasomòn. **Open** All year.

This imposing building is just in front of the superb cathedral of Burgos, on a small tiled square decorated with a pretty stone fountain, and has been the property of the same family for several generations. They first opened a well-known restaurant in a 15th-century house, the former printing shop of a disciple of Gutenberg. Decorated in the style of the period, a typically Castillian cuisine is served. In the newer hotel they have kept the most representative elements (woodwork and tiled floors) to recall the past. In fact, the rooms are more functional than elegan, and lack originality. Some of them overlook the cathedral while others look over the town roofs. The location is ideal for discovering the charms of Burgos, best known among other things for speaking the purest form of Castillian.

How to get there (Map 4): *facing the cathedral.*

Hotel Arlanza ★★★

09346 Covarrubias (Burgos)
Plaza Mayor, 11
Tel. (9)47-40 30 25 - Fax (9)47-40 63 59
Sr J. Ortiz Juarros

Rooms 38 and 2 suites with telephone, shower, and WC. **Price** Single 5,300Pts, double 9,000Pts. **Meals** Breakfast 650Pts, served 8:00-10.00; full board + 3,000Pts (per pers., 3 days min.). **Restaurant** Service 13:00-15:45, 20:30-22:45; closed Sun night, menus 2,700Pts. Specialties: Sopa serrana - Cordero. **Credit cards** Amex, Visa, Eurocard, MasterCard. **Pets** Dogs not allowed. **Facilities** Garage (1,000Pts). **Nearby** Collegiata de Covarrubias - Church Santa Maria in Quintanillas de la Viñas - Monastery Santo Domingo de Silos - Lerma - Burgos. **Open** 15. Mar - 15. Dec.

Simple and without pretentions, this hotel deserves its selection thanks to its superb siting: it dominates the square of Covarrubias, a charming Castillian village. The hotel is installed in a former noble's home and has been restored in a rustic style, and the interior refurbished with a desire for sobriety. The rooms would merit a rather brighter decor, and this is why we prefer those looking out from the facade as they are larger, and enjoy the view of the square. No sophisticated cuisine is served but good house dishes based on the produce of the area.

How to get there *(Map 4): 39km south of Burgos via N234, to Cuevas de San Clemente, then small road to Covarrubias.*

Hotel Tres Coronas de Silos ★★★

09610 Santo Domingo de Silos (Burgos)
Plaza Mayor, 6
Tel. (9)47-39 00 47 - Fax (9)47-39 00 65
Sr Martin

Rooms 16 with telephone, bath, and WC. **Price** Single 5,500-5,900Pts, double 8,700-9,200Pts. **Meals** Breakfast 850Pts, served 8:30-11:00; full board + 3,900Pts (per pers.). **Restaurant** Service 13:30-15:30, 20:30-23:30; carte 3,500-4,500Pts. Specialties: Morcillos - Jamón - Picadillo - Menestra de verduras naturales. **Credit cards** Amex, Visa, Eurocard, MasterCard. **Pets** Dogs allowed. **Nearby** Monastery Santo Domingo de Silos - Collegiata de Covarrubias - Salas de los Infantes - Caves of the Yecla. **Open** All year.

Santo Domingo de Silos is a very beautiful and very authentic Castillian village renowned for its convent dating from the year 1000 (note the very fine cloisters where one can hear the Gregorian chant every day). Opposite the main square and the church, a large 18th-century house restored by the local craftsmen has become this intimate family hotel. A charming dining room with a large wood-burning stove allows one to sample the house's regional cuisine. At the top of an attractive wooden staircase, the delightful and snug rooms match the Castillian style of the whole residence. The welcome is friendly and relaxed. If you cannot find the hotel ask for the Casa Grande (Big house), as it is known by the village people.

How to get there *(Map 4): 58km south of Burgos via N234 to Hacinas, then take the small road to Santo Domingo.*

Hospederia del Monasterio de Valvanera ★★

26322 Anguiano (La Rioja)
Tel. (9)41 37 70 44

Rooms 25 with shower, WC and TV. **Price** Single 3,500Pts, double 5,000Pts.
Meals Breakfast 400Pts, served 9:00-10:00; half board 1,600Pts, full board
+ 2,900Pts (per pers.). **Restaurant** Service 13.30-14.30, 20.30-21.30; menu
1,400Pts. Specialties: regional cooking. **Credit cards** Amex, Visa, Eurocard,
MasterCard. **Pets** Dogs not allowed. **Facilities** Parking. **Nearby** San Millàn de
la Cogolla - Santo Domingo de la Calzada. **Open** 8. Jan - 21. Dec.

At the peak of a very green mountain an immense red-stone
monastery looks out each evening on a real postcard sunset.
The hotel occupies the rear part of the monastery to which one
has access via the gallery-cloister. The architecture has remained
sumptuous, as it always was. The rooms are modest but very
clean. If you want to fill your lungs with good clean air in an
exceptional environment of beauty and peace, the Hospederia
del Monasterio de Valvanera is well worth a detour (by a very
difficult road as well). However, if you are looking for
comfortable and cossetted rooms it is better to drive on, for an
air of great sobriety reigns here: do not forget you are in a
monastery after all.

How to get there *(Map 5): 48km southwest of Logroño via N120 to
Nájera, then C113.*

C A S T I L L A   L E O N

Parador Marco Fabio ★★★

26500 Calahorra (La Rioja)
Era Alta - Quintiliano
Tel. (9)41-13 03 58 - Fax (9)41-13 51 39

Rooms 62 with telephone, bath, WC and minibar. **Price** Double 11,500Pts.
Meals Breakfast 1,200Pts, served 8:00-10:30; full board + 6,375Pts (per
pers.). **Restaurant** Service 13:00-15:30, 20:30-23:00; menu 3,200Pts, also à
la carte. Specialties: Cordero. **Credit cards** Amex, Visa, Eurocard, MasterCard.
Pets Dogs not allowed. **Facilities** Parking. **Nearby** Arnedo. **Open** All year.

This is a rather classical parador whose facade has an austere
aspect, but which is surrounded by a flowery terrace at the
back of the building. As in all paradors, the rooms are
particularly large and great use has been made of wood, which
gives them a warmer character. The furniture is classical and the
floor-tiles polished. Even if you are just passing through, do not
leave without visiting the town cathedral known as the
'Cathedral of the Sacristy'.

*How to get there (Map 5): 100km southwest of Pamplona via A15, then
A68 towards Logroño, exit Calahorra.*

85

Hotel Los Agustinos ★★★★

26200 Haro (La Rioja)
Calle San Agustin, 2
Tel.(9)41-31 13 08 – Fax (9)41-30 31 48
Sr de Miguel Luengo

Rooms 62 with air-conditioning, telephone, bath, WC, cable TV and minibar; elevator. **Price** Single 7,200-10,000Pts, double 9,300-12,500Pts. **Meals** Breakfast 975Pts, served 7:30-10:30; half board + 3,475 Pts, full board + 5,800Pts (per pers.). **Restaurant** Service 13:30-15:30, 20:30-23:00; closed Sun and Aug; carte 3,000-3,650Pts. Specialties: Patatas a la riojana - cordero. **Credit cards** All major. **Pets** Dogs allowed in the rooms. **Facilities** Parking. **Nearby** Villages of Briones, San Vicente de la Sonsierra and de Casalareina - Balcòn de Rioja. **Open** All year.

A 14th-century convent, and then a military hospital, prison, bus station and now a hotel, this is a real pleasure for us because the restoration here has been made with taste. Our greatest delight was in the terrace formed around the cloister, which is also the setting for a patio: the former torture chamber of the prison! (but be assured, the ambiance is all the same very happy!). The cloister arcades aligned the prisoners' cells and on the stonework one can still read their scribblings, which are sometimes very amusing. The church has become the lounge. As for the rooms, they are classical. The restaurant cellars offer a particularly wide choice of wines; the region is well qualified for this, to be sure. An excellent halting place for a trip through this area of renowned wines.

How to get there (Map 5): 90km south of Bilbao via A68.

Motel de Pradorrey ★★★

24700 Astorga (León)
Tel. (9)87-61 57 29 - Fax (9)87-61 92 20
Sr Sanchez

Rooms 64 with telephone, bath, WC, cable TV and minibar. **Price** Single 7,100-8,200Pts, double 10,000-11,300Pts, suite 11,000-12,300Pts. **Meals** Breakfast 700Pts, served 8:00-12:00; half board + 3,475 Pts, full board + 5,800Pts (per pers.). **Restaurant** With air-conditioning, service 13.00-16.00, 21.00-24.00; menu 2,000Pts. Specialties: Cames rojas - Embutidos. **Credit cards** All major. **Pets** Dogs allowed in the rooms. **Facilities** Parking. **Nearby** in Astorga: the cathedral - Monastery Santa Maria de Carrizo - La Bañeza - Church of Luyego - Castrillo de los Polvazares. **Open** All year.

At an altitude of 950 meters, the Motel de Pradorrey is housed in a medieval edifice that still bears on its facade, as well as inside, some vestiges of the constructions of the Templers' Order. The beauty of its stones and the wrought ironwork are remarkable but the interior is less attractive. Why sacrifice to comfort the charm one might have expected from admiring the hotel's outside ? This being said, the hotel is in a part of León that is a region still preserved from tourism, and where one can drive through some of the most typical villages of Spain, such as Castrillo de Los Polvazares. Three kilometers away, one can also visit the famous cathedral of Astorga. Please note, the hotel's restaurant has a good reputation.

How to get there *(Map 3): 52km west of León via N120, then N6 towards La Coruña.*

C A S T I L L A   L E O N

Parador Hostal San Marcos ★★★★★

24001 León
Plaza San Marcos, 7
Tel. (9)87-23 73 00 - Fax (9)87-23 34 58
Sr Alvarez Montoto

Rooms 256 with telephone, bath, WC, TV and minibar; elevator. **Price** Double 16,500-17,500Pts. **Meals** Breakfast 1,200Pts, served 7:45-11:30; full board + 6,970Pts (per pers.). **Restaurant** With air-conditioning, service 13:30-15:30, 21:00-23:30; menu 3,500Pts. Specialties: Trout "Hostal" - Cecina. **Credit cards** All major. **Pets** Dogs not allowed. **Facilities** Parking. **Nearby** in Leòn: Cathedral, Monastery San Marcos, Basilica San Isidoro - Monastery San Miguel de Escalada - Castle of Valencia of Don Juan - Caves of the Robla. **Open** All year.

No, this is not a museum entrance but it really is the hotel San Marcos! A historical monument, the former Santiaguista convent is the pride of the province of León. Its facade is a beautiful example of the 'plateresque' style, so called because of its resemblance to silver plate work. Inside, the massive and grandiose architecture of the cloister that surrounds the garden, is in contrast to the grace of the arches of the upper gallery, where tables are set out. A very beautiful lounge occupies the former chapter house with its astonishing 'mudejar' ceiling. There is unmatched comfort in all rooms, but naturally one prefers those of the main building as the annex has much less charm. An impeccable service and great friendliness are still the qualities of this classy hotel.

How to get there (Map 3): in the town center.

88

Hotel Castillo de Monzòn ★★★

34410 Monzòn de Campos (Palencia)
Tel. (9)79-80 80 75 - Fax (9)79-80 83 03

Rooms 9 and 1 suite with telephone, bath, WC and TV. **Price** Single 8,000Pts, double 13,000-28,600Pts. **Meals** Breakfast 850Pts, served 8:00-11:00; full board + 4,760Pts (per pers.). **Restaurant** Service 13:30-15:30, 20:30-23:30; menus 3,000-4,500Pts, also à la carte. Specialties: Meat, regional cooking. **Credit cards** Amex, Visa, Eurocard, MasterCard. **Pets** Dogs not allowed. **Facilities** Parking. **Nearby** in Monzòn: the church - Cathedral of Palencia - Ribas de Campos - Amusco - Piña de Campos - Tamara. **Open** All year.

The town of Monzòn is a former royal residence and it has converted its historic castle into a hotel. The arrival at this fortress on its small hill is impressive enough, with a very imposing building and its high tower and window-less walls. The interior however is welcoming and even if the architecture has been restored, the most attractive elements, such as a Roman arch and some beautiful ceilings, have been preserved. Comfort is also here in the rooms with their canopied beds and heavy drapes, to remind you that you are staying in a 'chateau'. In a rustic atmosphere, a fine restaurant offers good braised meats and an excellent menu of regional specialties. The hotel is isolated but in fact only eleven kilometers from Palencia, which has conserved a magnificent Gothic cathedral from its past and is well worth a visit. This is a most pleasant staging post.

How to get there (Map 4): 11km north of Palencia.

Hosterìa El Convento ★★

34492 Santa Maria de Mave (Palencia)
Tel. (9)79-12 36 11
Familia Moral

Rooms 25 with bath. **Price** Single 4,000Pts, double 6,000Pts, suite 8,000-10,000Pts. **Meals** Breakfast 350Pts, served 8:00-12:00; half board + 4,500 Pts, full board + 6,000Pts (per pers.). **Restaurant** Service 13:30-15:30, 20:30-22:30; menu 1,500Pts. Specialties: Sopa castillana - cordero. **Credit cards** Amex, Visa, Eurocard, MasterCard. **Pets** Dogs not allowed. **Facilities** Parking. **Nearby** Hunting and fishing - Aguilar de Campoò - Monastery de Santa Maria La Real. **Open** All year.

Between Santander and Palencia in a region rich in Roman ruins, this very beautiful medieval priory shelters a hotel run in the family style, and where the charming daughters of the house look after the reception. Attached to the building, a pretty church is still in use. Understandably the rooms respect the spirit of the house and have a rather monk-like aspect. Their furniture is restricted to the essential, their walls bare and the entry doors small, but the bathrooms contribute a more contemporary touch. A little more sophisticated, the suites have canopied beds. The main room of the restaurant, with its beams, stone walls and tiled floors, is cheered by pretty lighting and intimate tabling. It is with a great pleasure that you relax in the garden, and as your eyes wander out over the rocky canyon of the Horadada and the surrounding limestone formations. Peace and well-being are to be found here.

How to get there *(Map 4): 116km south of Santander, towards Palencia via N611.*

Hotel Rector ★★★★

37008 Salamanca
Paseo Rector Esperabé, 10
Tel. (9)23-21 84 82 – Fax (9)23-21 40 08
Sr Ferràn

Rooms 14 with air-conditioning, telephone, bath, WC, cable TV, safe and minibar; elevator. **Price** Single 10,000-12,000Pts, double 15,000Pts. **Meals** Breakfast 900Pts, served 8:00-11:00. **Restaurant** See p.199. **Credit cards** All major. **Pets** Dogs not allowed. **Facilities** Garage (700Pts). **Nearby** Castillo de Buen Amor - Peñaranda de Bracamonte - Ciudad Rodrigo - Candelario - La Alberca. **Open** All year.

The hotel is in a beautiful house of golden stone from the Villamayor region, like most of the other buildings in the town of Salamanca. Famous for its university, this is one of the most attractive towns in Spain. With a great wealth of monuments, it retains admirable remains from both the Renaissance and baroque periods, among them the Plaza Mayor, to name only one of them. The hotel has been fully renovated but with great refinement. The reception lounges on the ground floor have been made very light and airy. The furniture and chairs in mahogany and covered with salmon-pink fabrics, and assorted drapes give the decor an air of gentleness. Blue has been chosen for the rooms, which are very comfortable indeed, with their attractive bathrooms all in white marble. The hotel's small capacity ensures a very attentive service, along with a very friendly welcome. This is a very good staging post in a town that really deserves a visit.

How to get there *(Map 11): 205km northwest of Madrid via A63, towards Avila; at 98km from Avila, via N501.*

CASTILLA LEON

Parador Enrique II de Trastamara ★★★

37500 Ciudad Rodrigo (Salamanca)
Plaza del Castillo, 1
Tel. (9)23-46 01 50 – Fax (9)23-46 04 04
Sr Aliste Lopez

Rooms 27 with air-conditioning, telephone, bath, WC, TV and minibar. **Price** Single 8,000-10,000Pts, double 10,000-13,000Pts. **Meals** Breakfast 1,200Pts, served 8:00-10:30; full board + 6,375Pts (per pers. 2 days min.). **Restaurant** Service 13:00-16:00, 20:00-23:00; menu 3,200Pts, also à la carte. Specialties: regional cooking. **Credit cards** All major. **Pets** Dogs not allowed. **Facilities** Parking **Nearby** in Ciudad Rodrigo: the cathedral - Ruins of Urueña in Fuenteguinaldo - Villages: Peña de Francia and La Alberca. **Open** All year.

Ciudad Rodrigo is a fortified 12th-century town built on the orders of Fernando II. The chateau-alcazar that shelters the parador is in the center of the town on the banks of the River Agueda. As with many of these chateaux, their austere and rather severe side is relieved by beautiful flower gardens. The best rooms are those which, like the lounge and dining room, have a view of the river and town. Classified a historical monument, Ciudad Rodrigo well merits a visit.

How to get there (Map 11): 88km from Salamanca via N620, towards Portugal.

Hotel Infanta Isabel ★★★

40001 Segovia
Plaza Mayor Isabel la Catolica, 1
Tel. (9)21-44 31 05 – Fax (9)21-43 32 401
Sr E. Canada Cardo

Rooms 29 with air-conditioning, telephone, bath, WC, cable TV, safe and minibar; elevator. **Price** Single 7,000Pts, double 10,300-12,500Pts. **Meals** Breakfast 1,000Pts, served 8:30-11:00. **Restaurant** See p. 199. **Credit cards** All major. **Pets** Dogs not allowed. **Facilities** Garage (1,000Pts). **Nearby** in Segovia: Roman aqueduct, the cathedral, churches of San Martìn, San Millàn and San Estebàn (tower), Alcàzar, Monastery de El Parral - Turégano - Pedraza de la Sierra - Castle Castilnovo - Sepùlveda - Royal Palace of La Granja - Palacio de Riofrio. **Open** All year.

A royal city, Segovia is one of the most attractive towns in Spain, and one comes here to visit its architectural treasures and also sample the gastronomic specialties (trout and above all its sucking pig roasted over a wood fire), which have made its reputation. The hotel is admirably situated opposite the cathedral, and it is a charming little hotel full of elegance and refinement. Everything is in good taste: modern comforts, classical decor and impeccable service. Breakfast is delicious and the welcome most attentive. The rooms are enchanting, bright and quiet, and most have a view of the cathedral. This is a very attractive address.

How to get there *(Map 13): 87km northwest of Madrid.*

Los Linajes ★★★

40003 Segovia
Dr. Velasco, 9
Tel. (9)21-46 04 75 – Fax (9)21-46 04 79
Sr Borrequero

Rooms 55 with telephone, bath, WC, TV; elevator. **Price** Single 6,000-9,000Pts, double 8,350-10,500Pts, suite 11,000-13,500Pts. **Meals** Breakfast 750Pts, served 8:30-10:30. **Restaurant-snack** Service 12:30-14:00, 20:00-23:00; carte. **Credit cards** All major. **Pets** Dogs allowed. **Facilities** Garage (850Pts). **Nearby** in Segovia: Roman aqueduct, the cathedral, churches of San Martìn, San Millàn and San Estebàn (tower), Alcàzar, Monastery del El Parral - Turégano - Pedraza de la Sierra - Castle Castilnovo - Sepùlveda - Royal Palace of La Granja - Palacio de Riofrio. **Open** All year.

The principal feature of Los Linajes is its location right in the heart of the historical quarter of San Esteban, in the fortified sector of the old town. Segovia is one of the most ancient cities of Spain. In the past it was the former Arab capital and a royal city, which has left it with many superb remains that today make it one of the most visited cities in the country. To this may be added its gastronomic reputation. The hotel has conserved the facade of the former 11th-century palace but the interior is decorated in a rather impersonal and functional style. The rooms, however, are comfortable and located on the various floors, while the most attractive have terraces. Meals may be taken in the fresh air where one can enjoy a splendid view of the Parral Monastery. Facing the same direction, the swimming pool contributes a welcome freshness after the burning heat of the day.

How to get there *(Map 13): 87km northwest of Madrid.*

La Posada de Don Mariano ★★

40172 Pedraza della Sierra (Segovia)
Tel. (9)21-50 98 86 - Fax (9)21-50 98 87 - Sr Mariano

Rooms 18 with telephone, bath, WC and TV. **Price** Single 9,000Pts, double 11,000Pts, suite 16,000Pts. **Meals** Breakfast 950Pts, served 8:00-11:00. **Restaurant** Service 13:15-15:30, 20:00-22:00; menu 2,900Pts. Specialties: regional cooking. **Credit cards** All major. **Pets** Dogs not allowed. **Facilities** Parking. **Nearby** Segovia - Castle Castilnovo - Sepùlveda. **Open** All year.

Behind a discreet facade, La Posada de Don Mariano reveals a real jewel decorated throughout by the director of the Spanish version of 'House & Garden'. Pedraza is a small medieval village straight off a postcard, situated on a huge rock and surrounded by walls. Preserved admirably, you can admire aristocratic homes with their shields and arms, along with the Plaza Mayor and its porched houses. The owner of La Posada has created an original style based on the typical elements: Castilian ceramics, furniture from Andalusia and Extremadura, mixed with creations such as fabrics from Canovas found on the beds, curtains and wall hangings. The tones vary with the rooms. White, and with a superb canopied bed, number 101 is a magnificent marital chamber. Along the corridors and in the patio, a host of green plants create a charming atmosphere, which is never 'precious' or affected. In the restaurant the white-covered tables promise romantic 'tête-à-têtes' by candlelight. This is a true hotel of charm in a village that has attracted and inspired many an artist.

How to get there *(Map 13): 36km northeast of Segovia via N110 towards Soria until Matabuena, then Pedraza.*

Hotel Mesón Leonor ★★★

42005 Soria
Paseo del Mirón
Tel. (9)75-22 02 50 - Fax (9)75-22 99 53
Sr Heras Varea

Rooms 32 with telephone, bath or shower, WC, TV, safe and minibar. **Price** Single 5,450-5,800Pts, double 7,950-8,950Pts, "Special" 8,950-9,450Pts, suite 10,500-11,500Pts. **Meals** Breakfast 550Pts, served 8:00-11:00; half board + 2,450 Pts, full board + 3,700Pts (per pers.). **Restaurant** Service 13:00-16:00, 21:00-23:00; menu 1,900Pts, also à la carte. Specialties: Meat. **Credit cards** All major. **Pets** Dogs allowed in the rooms. **Facilities** Parking. **Nearby** in Soria: cathedral San Pedro, churches of Santo Domingo and of San Juan de Duero - Vinuesa - Agreda - Sierra de Urbión: road of Laguna Negra de Urbìon to Laguna egra de Neila. **Open** All year.

Soria is one of those towns from "Lands of Castille" about which Antonio Machado has spoken so well. The large house sheltering the hotel is austere, while the interior is in Castilian style. The rooms however are more welcoming and comfortable; some of them, with mezzanines, are more spacious and will cost you a few extra pesetas. This is a very pleasant halt for those planning to walk in the beautiful Sierra de Urbìon.

How to get there (Map 5): 106km south of Logroño via N3.

Parador Rey Fernando II de León ★★★★

49600 Benavente (Zamora)
Paseo de Ramon y Cajal
Tel. (9)88-63 03 00 - Fax (9)88-63 03 03
Sra Lechuga Arribas

Rooms 30 with air-conditioning, telephone, bath, WC, TV and minibar. **Price** Double 11,500-12,000Pts. **Meals** Breakfast 1,200Pts, served 8:00-11:00; half board + 4,081 Pts, full board + 6,375Pts (per pers. 2 days min.). **Restaurant** Service 13:00-16:00, 20:30-23:00; menu 3,000Pts, also à la carte. Specialties: regional cooking. **Credit cards** All major. **Pets** Dogs not allowed. **Facilities** Garage (750Pts). **Nearby** Villalpando - Monastery of Moreruela - Church ofe Santa María de Tera. **Open** All year.

Built in the 12th-century, this chateau was the residence of King Fernando II who installed his court here in 1176. But after so many centuries it was practically destroyed during some battle between the French and English. Only the imposing Torre del Caraco remains today. To install the parador, it was thus necessary to build one wing for the rooms and a second for the dining room and reception. The lounge has been placed in the tower, whose main decorative element is the magnificent 'mudejar' ceiling in wood marquetry. In the TV room it was a good idea to make a mosaic from all the ceramic pieces found on the site. Apart from the comfort, one can also appreciate the terraces with their splendid panorama of the countryside.

How to get there (Map 3): 69km south of León via N630.

CASTILLA LEON

Parador Condes de Alba de Aliste ★★★★

49001 Zamora
Plaza Viriato, 5
Tel. (9)88-51 44 97 - Fax (9)88-53 00 63
Sra Pelegrín

Rooms 27 with telephone, bath, WC, TV and minibar; elevator. **Price** Single 9,600Pts, double 12,500-13,500Pts, suite 14,000Pts. **Meals** Breakfast 1,200Pts, served 8:00-10:30; full board 6,375Pts (per pers.). **Restaurant** service 13:00-16:00, 20:30-23:00; menu 3,200Pts, also à la carte. Specialties: Castilian cooking. **Credit cards** All major. **Pets** Dogs not allowed. **Facilities** Swimming pool, garage. **Nearby** in Zamora: the cathedral, Museo Catedralicio (Flamencos tapestries) - Church at Arcenillas - Church at San Pedro de la Nave - Colegiata de Toro. **Open** All year.

This 15th-century palace is right in the heart of Zamora on the edge of the old quarter. Largely destroyed during the revolt of the 'Comuneros' in the 16th century, it was then restored by the Counts of Alba and of Aliste, and later became a hospital in the 18th century. The magnificent Renaissance cloister still survives today, along with a double gallery, the balcony, and the grand monumental staircase at the foot of which one can admire a superb coat of arms. Lounges and dining room succeed each other to the garden with its swimming pool. The rooms are very well furnished but the suite, facing the square, deserves a special mention for its comfort and reasonable price. The personnel are friendly and the lady director charming, and they do everything to ensure that your stay is one of the happiest times of your journey.

How to get there (Map 11): 62km north of Salamanca via N630.

98

Hosterìa Real de Zamora ★★★★

49000 Zamora
Cuesta de Pizarro, 7
Tel. (9)88-53 45 45 - Fax (9)88-53 45 22
Sr Loreto Dominguez

Rooms 16 with telephone, bath or shower, WC, TV and minibar. **Price** Single 4,780-5,580Pts, double 6,000-7,000Pts. **Meals** Breakfast 450Pts, served 8:00-10:00; half board 5,437Pts, full board 6,747 (per pers. 3 days min.). **Restaurant** "Pizarro" service 14:00-16:00, 21:00-23:30; menu 1,975Pts, also à la carte. Specialties: Basque and Castille cooking. **Credit cards** All major. **Pets** Dogs allowed. **Facilities** Parking. **Nearby** in Zamora: the cathedral, Museo Catedralicio (Flamencos tapestries) - Church at Arcenillas - Church at San Pedro de la Nave - Colegiata de Toro. **Open** 1. Mar - 31. Jan.

The hotel occupies a former palace of the Inquisition, itself built on an earlier Jewish building that legend links with the famous discoverer of Peru, Pizarro. A beautiful stone staircase leads to the rooms arranged around a pretty patio. Some of them, the largest, have a view of the River Ebro: the only nuisance is the noise from the street, but other rooms look onto the patio. All are attractive and fresh with their tiled floors and light walls. The bathrooms are without reproach and some astonishing ancient Jewish baths have been conserved; while the water comes from natural rock sources. Via a small staircase one reaches the garden and a terrace up against the medieval walls of the town, and here one can look out over the river. During Holy Week a series of classical music recitals is given in the patio or the beautiful restaurant room.

How to get there (Map 11): 62km north of Salamanca via N630.

99

C A S T I L L A   M A N C H A

Parador de la Mancha ★★★

02000 Albacete
Al Sureste
Tel. (9)67-22 94 50 - Fax (9)67-22 60 92
Sr Cornero Fandiño

Rooms 69 with air-conditioning, telephone, bath, WC, TV and minibar. **Price** Single 8,000Pts, double 10,500Pts. **Meals** Breakfast 1,100Pts, served 8:00-10:30; half board + 4,000Pts, full board + 5950Pts (per pers., 3 days min.). **Restaurant** Service 13:00-16:00, 20:30-23:00; menu: 3,000Pts, also à la carte. Specialties: Bacalão a la manchega - Pimientos rellenos - Pierna de cabrito al romero. **Credit cards** All major. **Pets** Dogs not allowed. **Facilities** Swimming pool, tennis, parking. **Nearby** in Albacete: Archeological Museum (Roman ivory dolls), Feria (September) - Alcaraz. **Open** All year

A good staging post towards the coast if coming from Madrid, or a starting point for discovering the vast plain of La Mancha, the setting for Don Quixote's adventures. The Parador de la Mancha will meet your needs as it is a comfortable hotel in the style of the country, built around a large patio with its fountain. One feels good in the large fresh rooms, each with its own small terrace. The swimming pool is always welcome in summer, while one will also appreciate the hotel's cuisine and getting to know the specialties of La Mancha, famous among other things for its cheese.

How to get there *(Map 11): 183km southwest of Valencia via N430, and 5km from Albacete.*

Parador de Almagro ★★★★

13270 Almagro (Ciudad Real)
Ronda de San Francisco
Tel. (926)-86 01 00 – Fax (926) 86-01 50
Sr Muñoz Romera

Rooms 55 with air-conditioning, telephone, bath, WC, TV and minibar. **Price** Double 12,000-13,500Pts. **Meals** Breakfast 1,200Pts, served 8:00-10:30; full board + 6,375Pts (per pers.). **Restaurant** Service 13:30-16:00, 21:00-23:00; menu: 3,200Pts, also à la carte. Specialties: Pisto manchego - Mojete - Migas. **Credit cards** All major. **Pets** Dogs not allowed. **Facilities** Swimming pool, tennis, parking. **Nearby** in Almagro: Plaza Mayor - Bolaños de Calatrava - Church of Moral de Calatrava - Calzada de Calatrava - National Park of Lagunas de Ruidera. **Open** All year.

The parador is built on the ancient convent of San Francisco (1506). Almagro rises out of the vast La Mancha plain and is a key staging post on the route of Cervantès. It is the town of lace and the center of the Order of Calatrava. It is also interesting for its Plaza Mayor, which is a real jewel with its extensive uninterrupted glazed windows, and the Corral de Comedias, the only surviving theater of the Siglo de Oro. The parador has no less than sixteen patios with galleries, where the flowers and fountains combine to create a magic atmosphere. Terra-cottas and faiences are often used in decorating the pretty rooms and the magnificent cellar next to the bar. The hotel is right in the heart of town, and has private parking, while the service is very good.

How to get there (Map 21): 22km east of Ciudad Real via C415.

CASTILLA MANCHA

Parador Marqués de Villena ★★★★

16213 Alarcón (Cuenca)
Avenida Amigos del Castillo
Tel. (9)66-33 13 50 – Fax (9)66-33 11 07
Sr Lopez

Rooms 13 with telephone, bath, WC, TV and minibar; elevator. **Price** Double 14,000-15,000Pts. **Meals** Breakfast 1,200Pts, served 8:15-11:00; full board + 5,950Pts (per pers.). **Restaurant** Service 13:15-16:00, 21:00-23:00; menu: 3,200Pts, also à la carte. Specialties: Bacalão a la Manchega. **Credit cards** All major. **Pets** Dogs not allowed. **Facilities** Parking. **Nearby** Motilla del Palancar - Valverde - Minglanilla - Puebla del Salvador - Yémeda. **Open** All year.

The parador is in the chateau of the little fortified town of Alarcón, and it seems to be the most beautiful and best conserved in the province of Cuenca. Set on the edge of the town on a huge rock almost entirely surrounded by the River Jucar, it enjoys a perfect tranquility. The rooms are pleasantly decorated and the bathrooms comfortable. Go for those in the tower, for even if they are rather sombre; their tiny windows, or sometimes loopholes, give them an added attraction. A special mention goes to Room 105, from which you can walk onto the circular pathway with its unmatched view over the surrounding country. Breakfast is perfect, particularly generous and excellent, and served in the imposing restaurant hall.

How to get there (Map 20): 85km south of Cuenca via N320 to Motilla del Palencar, then N3 towards Madrid.

102

Posada de San José ★★

16001 Cuenca
Calle Julián Romero, 4
Tel. (9)69-21 13 00 - Fax (9)69-23 03 65
Sra Morter y Sr Cortinas

Rooms 30 (21 with bath) **Price** 2,200-4,600Pts with 'lavabo', 3,800-8,900Pts with bath. **Meals** Breakfast 450Pts, served 8:00-11:00. **Bar-Restaurant** Service 17:30-22:30; closed Mon; carte. Specialties: Tapas, morteruedo, trucha escabechada. **Credit cards** All major. **Pets** Dogs allowed in the rooms. **Nearby** in Cuenca: the cathedral, las Casas Colgadas (Hanging Houses), Museo de Arte Abstractado (Museum of Spanish Abstract Art) - La Ciudad Encantada (Enchanted City) - Las Torcas - Hoz del Huecar (views). **Open** All year.

The posada occupies the former residence of the painter Martinez del Mazo, which is now a hotel full of charm with a magnificent view over the cliffs and vegetable gardens. Cuenca has been celebrated since the 14th century for its houses suspended above the Júcar gorges and, more recently, for its modern art museum. You will like this hotel for its simplicity and the comfortable rooms (apart from Number 9 with its 'lavabo'), and all are imbued with that same atmosphere of a well run house. The furniture and floor-tiles are well-polished, the curtains stitched by the seamstresses of Cuenca, cotton napkins and towels, and so on. Those rooms with bathrooms also have a beautiful view, while Rooms 15, 21, 32 and 33 also have terraces. A pretty garden and a friendly welcome are good reasons for choosing this posada, which also offers very reasonable prices.

How to get there *(Map 14): 63km southeast of Madrid.*

Hotel Cueva del Fraile

16001 Cuenca
Hoz del Huecar
Tel. (9)69-21 15 71 - Fax (9)69-25 60 47
Sr de la Torre

Rooms 63 with telephone, bath, WC and TV. **Price** Single 5,900-8,500Pts, double 7,500-13,900Pts. **Meals** Breakfast 795Pts, served 8:00-11:00; half board + 2,770Pts, full board + 4,033Pts (per pers.). **Restaurant** Service 13:00-16:00, 20:00-23:00; menu 1,975Pts, also à la carte. Specialties: regional cooking. **Credit cards** All major. **Pets** Dogs not allowed. **Facilities** Swimming pool, tennis (350Pts), parking. **Nearby** in Cuenca: the cathedral, las Casas Colgadas (Hanging Houses), Museo de Arte Abstractado (Museum of Spanish Abstract Art) - La Ciudad Encantada (Enchanted City) - Las Torcas. **Open** All year.

It is seven kilometers from Cuenca, in the midst of mountainous outcrops, that the 'Cueva del Fraile' is to be found. Before being converted some ten years ago into a welcoming and quiet hotel, this 15th-century building was first a convent and then a farm. The rooms are nothing extraordinary as their Castilian furnishings and lighting are not very welcoming. The most attractive are those reached via the covered gallery and overlooking the pretty interior courtyard. One will appreciate the dining room with its large open fireplace, or the bar with its mezzanine, for their rustic atmosphere. A friendly welcome and quality regional cuisine add to the charm of this peaceful establishment without any pretentions.

How to get there *(Map 14): 170km southeast of Madrid to Cuenca, then the road to Palomera for 6km, then to the left on the road to Buenache for 1.2km.*

104

Parador de Sigüenza ★★★

19003 Sigüenza (Guadalajara)
Tel. (9)66-33 13 50 - Fax (9)66-33 11 07
Sr Lopez

Rooms 77 with air-conditioning, telephone, bath, WC, TV and minibar; elevator. **Price** Double 14,000-15,500Pts. **Meals** Breakfast 1,200Pts, served 8:15-11:00; full board + 6,375Pts (per pers.). **Restaurant** Service 13:15-16:00, 20:30-22:30; menu: 3,200Pts, also à la carte. Specialties: regional cooking. **Credit cards** All major. **Pets** Dogs not allowed. **Facilities** Parking. **Nearby** in Sigüenza: the cathedral (Tomb of Don Martìn Vàsquez de Arca in the Chapel of the Doncel, the sacristy, Chapel of Santa Librada) - Village of Medinaceli. **Open** All year

At the summit of the fortified town of Sigüenza, which rises in terraces on the side of the hill, stands the imposing Moorish fortress which became a Bishop's Palace, and now a parador. The restoration and reconstruction work has been careful to respect the proportions of this enormous four-sided building of 7,000 m2. To soften the austerity of the site, courtyards and gardens have been laid out, while two immense rooms shelter the lounge and dining room with their sober Castilian furniture. The rooms, whether giving onto the courtyard or valley, are all comfortable while some have terraces with long reclining chairs. From the large tiled courtyard one has a magnificent view over the pink roofs of Sigüenza, and one can trace out the maze of tiny streets. In the marvellous cathedral do not miss the funeral monument of Doncel, from the 15th century, and one of the most beautiful sculptures in the history of Spanish art.

How to get there (Map 13): 130km northeast of Madrid; at 70km from Guadalajara via N11 to Alcolea del Pinar, then C204 towards Sigüenza.

Parador de Oropesa ★★★★

45460 Oropesa (Toledo)
Paza del Palacio, 1
Tel. (9)25-43 00 00 - Fax (9)25-43 07 77

Rooms 48 with air-conditioning, telephone, bath, WC, cable TV and minibar; elevator. **Price** Double 14,000-15,000Pts. **Meals** Breakfast 1,200Pts, served 8:00-10:30; full board + 5,950Pts (per pers.). **Restaurant** Service 13:00-16:00, 20:00-23:00; menu: 3,500Pts, also à la carte. Specialties: Cordero del campo - Perdiz de tiro a la toledana. **Credit cards** All major. **Pets** Dogs not allowed. **Facilities** Parking. **Nearby** "Ceramic road" from Talavera de la Reina, via Puente de Arzobispo, Valdeverdeja - Lake of Azutàn - Lagartera. **Open** All year.

The magnificent feudal 'château' of Oropesa was the first historic building to be converted into a parador in 1930. This is a superb gothic-mudejar building, square in plan, and flanked with towers and keeps that look out over the valley of the Campo Arañuelo, with the plain of Gredos in the far distance. It shares the site with a renaissance palace that one can visit. In the interior the large forms and original floors have been preserved, which give a lot of charm and character to the well-furnished reception rooms. The rooms have all the comforts of a grand hotel and terraces, some of which look over the valley. At the foot of the historic building is a magnificent swimming pool, bordered by lawns, which also offers a superb panorama. A very beautiful address that should not be missed.

How to get there *(Map 12): 70km southwest of Madrid via N401; close to the Puerta de Bisagra.*

Hostal del Cardenal ★★★

45004 Toledo
Paseo de Recaredo, 24
Tel. (9)25-22 49 00 - Fax (9)25-22 29 91
Sr Gonzalez Martín

Rooms 27 with air-conditioning, telephone, bath, WC, cable TV and minibar (suite). **Price** Single 6,675Pts, double 10,800Pts, suite 15,000Pts. **Meals** Breakfast 765Pts, served 7:15-11:00 **Restaurant** Service 13:15-16:00, 20:30-23:00; closed 24. Dec; carte 3,300-4,000Pts. Specialties: Cochinillo y cordero asado - Sopa de ajo - Perdiz estofado a la toledana. **Credit cards** All major. **Pets** Dogs allowed. **Facilities** Swimming pool, parking. **Nearby** in Toledo: Cathedral, Church of Santo Tomé ("El Entierro del Conte de Orgaz" by Greco), El Trànsito Synagogue, Museum of Santa Cruz - Aranjuez - "Don Quixote country": (N301,south of Aranjuez): Consuegra, Corral de Almaguer, Quintanar de la Orden, El Toboso, Mota del Cuervo Belmonte, Tomelloso, Argamasilla de Alba. **Open** All year.

In Toledo there are many reasons for staying at the Hostal del Cardenal: Its location, in the heart of the imperial city, facing the Puerta de Bisagra, one of the jewels of Toledo. Its site in a Toledan palace of the 18th century, former summer residence of Cardinal Lorenzana, archbishop of the city. The calm of its Moorish gardens where only the birdsong and fountains are to be heard. Its comfort and good cuisine, its summer dinners in the garden. And for a last evening stroll around the circular pathway of the 11th-century bastion of walls.

How to get there (Map 13): 70km south of Madrid via N401; near to the Porte de Bisagra.

Hotel Residencia La Almazara ★★

45080 Toledo
Carret de Cuerva
Tel. (9)25-22 38 66 – Fax (9)25-25 05 62
Sr Villamor

Rooms 21 with telephone, bath and WC. **Price** Single 3,200Pts, double 5,000-5,900Pts. **Meals** Breakfast 450Pts, served 8:00-11:00. **Restaurant** See p. 200. **Credit cards** All major. **Pets** Dogs not allowed. **Facilities** Parking. **Nearby** in Toledo: Cathedral, Church of Santo Tomé (El Entierro del Conte de Orgaz od Greco), El Trànsito Synagogue, Museum of Santa Cruz - Aranjuez - "Don Quixote country": (N301, south of Aranjuez): Consuegra, Corral de Almaguer, Quintanar de la Orden, El Toboso, Mota del Cuervo Belmonte, Tomelloso, Argamasillo de Alba **Open** 6. Mar - 11. Dec.

Protected by 500 hectares of olive trees, oaks and junipers, this hotel was the former vacation home of Cardinal Quiroza in the 16th century. It is the oldest hotel in the city and it featured in the El Greco painting, 'General view of Toledo'. The rooms are simple but very attractive with their brand new bathrooms. Rooms 1 to 9 also have terraces with a breathtaking view. The countryside around and the softness of the light make this place a real haven that one is always happy to return to after a tiring visit to Toledo or its surroundings.

How to get there *(Map 13): 73.5km south of Madrid to Toledo via N401; then 3.5km on the road to Arges, near to the restaurant Monterrey-Aire de Cigarrales*

Parador Conde de Orgaz ★★★★

45001 Toledo
Cerro del Emperador
Tel. (9)25-22 18 50 - Fax (9)25-22 51 66
Sr Molina Aranda

Rooms 76 with air-conditioning, telephone, bath, WC, TV and minibar; elevator.
Price Double 15,000-16,000Pts. **Meals** Breakfast 1,200Pts, served 8:00-10:30;
full board + 6,970Pts (per pers., 2 days min.). **Restaurant** Service 13:00-16:00,
20:30-23:00; menu 3,500Pts, also à la carte. Specialties: Duelos y quebrantos -
Perdiz a la toledana - Ponche toledano. **Credit cards** All major. **Pets** Dogs not
allowed. **Facilities** Swimming pool, parking. **Nearby** in Toledo: Cathedral, Church
of Santo Tomé ("El Entierro del Conte de Orgaz" Greco), El Trànsito Synagogue,
Museum of Santa Cruz - Aranjuez - "Don Quixote country": (N301,south of
Aranjuez): Consuegra, Corral de Almaguer, Quintanar de la Orden, El Toboso,
Mota del Cuervo Belmonte, Tomelloso, Argamasillo de Alba. **Open** All year.

The parador, which takes its name from the famous painting
by El Greco, 'The burial of the Count of Orgaz', is on the
'Emperor's Hill', in the privileged quarter of Cigarrales. This
quarter dominates Toledo and offers an unmatched view
between the Alcántara and San Martin bridges. This remarkable
site has conditioned the layout of the buildings. With its
completely Toledan character, the hotel is very comfortable and
air-conditioned, and also has a swimming pool, both major
'pluses' when visiting Toledo in summer.

*How to get there (Map 13): 70km south of Madrid via N401; facing the
city on the other side of the River Tagus (Tajo).*

Hotel Domenico ★★★★

45002 Toledo
Cerro del Emperador
Tel. (9)25-25 00 40 - Fax (9)25-25 28 77
Sr R. Vidales Sànchez-Infantes

Rooms 48 and 2 suites with air-conditioning, telephone, bath, WC, cable TV, safe and minibar; elevator. **Price** Single 10,000Pts, double 12,000-14,000Pts, 3 pers. 16,000Pts, 4 pers. 14,000-20,000Pts. **Meals** Breakfast 1,000Pts, served 8:00-10:30; half board + 4,000Pts, full board + 6,000Pts (per pers., 2 days min.). **Restaurant** Service 13:00-16:00, 20:30-23:00, menu 3,000Pts, also à la carte. Specialties: regional cooking. **Credit cards** All major. **Pets** Dogs not allowed. **Facilities** Swimming pool, parking. **Nearby** in Toledo: Cathedral, Church of Santo Tomé ("El Entierro del Conte de Orgaz" Greco), El Trànsito Synagogue, Museum of Santa Cruz - Aranjuez - "Don Quixote country": (N301, south of Aranjuez): Consuegra, Corral de Almaguer, Quintanar de la Orden, El Toboso, Mota del Cuervo Belmonte, Tomelloso, Argamasillo de Alba. **Open** All year.

The Hotel Domenico is not in the town center but on the high ground close by, which allows you to admire this ancient city as El Greco painted it. The architecture of the hotel has all the rigor of the arid mineral countryside surrounding it. The hotel interior is very ordinary, the decor modern but without style, but all the rooms have terraces offering magnificent views over the countryside and, even better, over the old town. The lounge and bar are very lively areas, while the swimming pool with its shady corner terraces is much appreciated. The site, services and quality of facilities all quickly make you forget the banality of the decor.

How to get there *(Map 13): 70km south of Madrid via N401; facing the town on the other bank of the Tagus.*

Hotel Ritz ★★★★★

08010 Barcelona
Gran Via de les Corts Catalanes, 668
Tel. (9)3-318 52 00 – Fax (9)3-318 01 48
Sr Torres

Rooms 150 and 12 suites with air-conditioning, telephone, bath, WC, cable TV, safe and minibar; elevator. **Price** Single 32,800-41,500Pts, double 43,000-52,000Pts, suite 126,000Pts. **Meals** Breakfast 2,300Pts, served 7:00-11:00; half board + 4,200Pts. **Restaurant** Service 13:30-16:00, 20:30-23:00; carte 5,500Pts. Specialties: Pollo con langostinas - Escudella i carn d'olla. **Credit cards** All major. **Pets** Dogs not allowed. **Facilities** Parking. **Nearby** Sitges (beach) - Monastery of San Cugat del Valle - Montserrat - Vich; Prat golf course (9-and 18-Hole), San Cugat golf course (18-Hole). **Open** All year.

Since its opening in 1919, time has not tarnished its image, as one would expect from 'The Ritz'. The building and its interior are very splendid: from the entrance, the grand double staircase, the main hallway and all the attention you are given do not deceive, you are in a real palace. The rooms are more impersonal even if all are very comfortable. The hotel restaurant offers international cuisine but also a good variety of Catalan dishes. The terrace of the small interior garden is also a pleasant spot for having a drink, while a visit to the bar in the basement is obligatory.

How to get there *(Map 8): on the 'Diagonal'; close to the Plaza de Catalunya.*

Hotel Méridien Barcelone ★★★★

08002 Barcelona
Ramblas, 111
Tel. (9)3-318 62 00 - Fax (9)3-301 77 76

Rooms 209 with air-conditioning, telephone, bath, WC, cable TV, video and minibar; elevator; handicap access. **Price** Single 23,000Pts, double 29,000Pts, suite 68,000Pts. **Meals** Breakfast 2,100Pts, served 8:00-11:30. **Restaurant** Service 13:00-16:00, 20:00-24:00; menu 3,600Pts. Specialties: Catalan cooking. **Credit cards** All major. **Pets** Dogs not allowed. **Facilities** Garage. **Nearby** Sitges (beach) - Monastery of San Cugat del Valle - Montserrat - Vich; Prat golf course (9 and 18-Hole), San Cugat golf course (18-Hole). **Open** All year.

Here again the 'Ramblas' has been chosen to modernize an old hotel. The services are those of a grand hotel intended for a clientele of wealthy tourists or businessmen. One must however recognize the special effort that has been made in matters of decor. The lounges are luxurious. The rooms with their immense beds are furnished in the style of the 1930's, with an abundance of fabrics in soft colors that create an elegant and subtle atmosphere. If you would like to reserve a suite, then ask for 918. This is a hotel to stay to see the lights of the town, while also profiting from its voluptuous comfort. The interesting rates for weekends should be noted.

How to get there (Map 8): in the old city.

Hotel Duques de Bergara ★★★★

08002 Barcelona
Calle Bergara, 11
Tel. (9)3-301 51 51 - Fax (9)3-317 34 42
Sra M. Jané

Rooms 56 with air-conditioning, telephone, bath, WC, cable TV and minibar; elevator. **Price** Single 13,500Pts, double 14,900Pts. **Meals** Breakfast 1,200Pts, served 7:00-10:30. **Restaurant** Service 13:00-16:00, 20:00-24:00; menu 1,800Pts. Specialties: international cooking. **Credit cards** All major. **Pets** Dogs not allowed. **Nearby** Sitges (beach) - Monastery of San Cugat del Valle - Montserrat - Vich; Prat golf course (9-and 18-Hole), San Cugat golf course (18-Hole). **Open** All year.

This is a private house built in 1903 and converted into a hotel a few years ago. The entrance is beautiful enough to take your breath away: its 'caisson' ceiling of incredible height opens onto a glass roof that fills the hotel with the sort of light that photographers dream about. Marble covers all the staircase right up to the magnificent doors. Alas, like almost all older hotels trying to keep abreast of the demands of the modern visitor, nothing in the bedrooms recalls the past of such an attractive building. This being said, even if they are modern, it does not make them any less pleasant. The bathrooms are specially functional. The dining room, although sadly neglected, is still a comfortable staging post that deserves noting.

How to get there (Map 8): on the 'Diagonal'.

Hotel Condes de Barcelona ★★★★

08008 Barcelona
Paseo de Gracia, 75
Tel. (9)3-488 22 00 – Fax (9)3-488 06 14

Rooms 183 with air-conditioning, telephone, bath, WC, cable TV, video and minibar; elevator. **Price** Double 13,500 (week-end)-29,000Pts, suite "Gaudi" 20,000 (week-end)-34,000Pts, suite "Barcelona"30,000 (week-end)-58,000Pts. **Meals** Breakfast 1,270Pts, served 7:00-11:00; half board + 4,400Pts, full board + 8,400Pts. **Restaurant** Service 13:00-22:30; menu 4,400Pts, also à la carte. Specialties: Catalan and international cooking. **Credit cards** All major. **Pets** Dogs not allowed. **Facility** Swimming pool, garage (1,500Pts). **Nearby** Sitges (beach) - Monastery of San Cugat del Valle - Montserrat - Vich; Prat golf course (9-and 18-Hole), San Cugat golf course (18-hole). **Open** All year.

A few meters away from the famous house of Gaudi, "La Pedrera", there stood another 'Art Nouveau' house, "La Casa Batllo," which is now one of the best hotels in Barcelona. The interior architecture is very pure, with modern black furniture, halogen lighting, and a very refined setting for a select clientele patronizing the lounges and bar. Whatever the layout of the rooms, they are comfortable: those on the courtyard look out onto a beautiful terrace and gardens; the rooms on the street are well insulated from the noise; and in the older building all those on the upper floor have been renovated. We recommend the Gaudi or Barcelona suites. Very fashionable and a little bit sophisticated, yet no way pretentious.

How to get there (Map 8): on the 'Diagonal'; Plaza de Catalunya, then Paseo de Gracia.

Hotel Rivoli Rambla ★★★★

08002 Barcelona
Rambla dels Estudis, 128
Tel. (9)3-302 66 43 - Fax (9)3-317 50 53
Sr Paradela

Rooms 89 with air-conditioning, telephone, bath, WC, cable TV, safe and minibar; elevator; handicap access. **Price** Single and double 14,000 (week-end)-18,000Pts, suite 21-27,000 (week-end)-29-36,000Pts. **Meals** Breakfast 1,600Pts (buffet), served 7:00-11:00. **Restaurant** Service 13:00-15:00, 20:30-23:00; carte. Specialties: Fideua - Arroz negre - Paëlla. **Credit cards** All major. **Pets** Dogs not allowed. **Facilities** Swimming pool, sauna (2,500Pts), health center (2,000Pts), Jacuzzi (4,000Pts), garage (1,900Pts). **Nearby** Sitges (beach) - Monastery of San Cugat del Valle - Montserrat - Vich; Prat golf course (9-and 18-Hole), San Cugat golf course (18-Hole). **Open** All year.

A modern hotel that also has charm is not so very common. Lounges and rooms have mostly been furnished in the 1930's style, and the colors have been given particular attention. A certain number of 'trompe-l'oeils' have been painted on columns and walls. In the dining room a lot of interesting paintings have been hung to warm up the atmosphere. The halogen lighting is very soft and all is very silent. The rooms are large enough, with a deep grey moquette speckled with red. The hotel also offers suites, and the most attractive is the Opéra suite, with its jacuzzi-equipped bathroom. The welcome is most attentive.

How to get there (Map 8): in the old city.

115

Astoria Hotel ★★★

08036 Barcelona
Calle Paris, 203
Tel. (9)3-209 83 11 - Fax (9)3-202 30 08

Rooms 114 with air-conditioning, telephone, bath or shower, WC, cable TV, safe and minibar; elevator. **Price** Single 8,800 (week-end)-12,100Pts, double 8,000 (week-end)-13,800Pts. **Meals** Breakfast 1,100Pts, served 7:00-10:30. **Restaurant** See pp. 201-203. **Credit cards** All major. **Pets** Dogs not allowed. **Facilities** Parking. **Nearby** Sitges (beach) - Monastery of San Cugat del Valle - Montserrat - Vich; Prat golf course (9-and 18-Hole), San Cugat golf course (18-Hole). **Open** All year.

This beautiful hotel with its Art-Deco facade, even though only built in the 1950's, is in the residential quarter of Barcelona, the Estoril. A very solemn hallway, marble columns and large mirrors all set the tone. The rooms are double-glazed and decorated simply, but offer all the comforts. In the bathrooms some elements have been covered with marble. There is no restaurant but a bar with pleasant lamps has a snug atmosphere, along with an attractive rest lounge. The general ambiance is discreet and elegant.

How to get there (Map 8): on the 'Diagonal'.

Hotel Colón ★★★★

08002 Barcelona
Avenida de la Catedral, 7
Tel. (9)3-301 14 04 - Fax (9)3-317 29 15
Sr Gretz Badia

Rooms 147 with air-conditioning, telephone, bath, WC, TV and minibar; elevator. **Price** Single 13,750Pts, double 20,500Pts, suite 32,500-37,000Pts. **Meals** Breakfast 1,500Pts (buffet), served 7:00-11:00; half board + 4,800Pts, full board + 6,480Pts. **Restaurant** Service 13:00-15:00, 20:00-23:30; menu 3,300Pts, also à la carte. Specialties: Catalan and international cooking. **Credit cards** All major. **Pets** Dogs allowed. **Nearby** Sitges (beach) - Monastery of San Cugat del Valle - Montserrat - Vich; Prat golf course (9 and 18-Hole), San Cugat golf course (18-Hole). **Open** All year.

The Hotel Colón has an unequaled site: in the heart of the gothic quarter and facing the 13th-century cathedral. This is an institution for foreign tourists, and even if some fittings and equipment are now rather dated, it still remains a very agreeable hotel to live in. The ambiance is cosy, as with any good old hotel, making the lounges and bar a nice place to visit in the evenings. The rooms vary but one goes first for those on the top floor with their superb terraces. With the 'Ramblas' a few paces away, this is the ideal spot in Barcelona!

How to get there (Map 8): *facing the cathedral.*

Hotel Regencia Colón ★★★

08002 Barcelona
Avenida de la Catedral, 7
Tel. (9)3-318 98 58 - Fax (9)3-317 28 22
Sr Gretz Badia

Rooms 55 with air-conditioning, telephone, bath or shower, WC, TV, safe and minibar; elevator. **Price** Single 8,900Pts, double 15,500Pts, triple 19,000Pts. **Meals** Breakfast included (buffet), served 7:00-11:00. **Restaurant** See pp 201-203. **Credit cards** All major. **Pets** Dogs allowed. **Facilities** Parking (2,200Pts). **Nearby** Sitges (beach) - Monastery of San Cugat del Valle - Montserrat - Vich; Prat golf course (9 and 18-Hole), San Cugat golf course (18-Hole). **Open** All year.

Situated just next to its 'big brother', the Regencia Colón is very much less expensive but offers the same convenient site, along with comfortable and well equiped rooms. Nothing is very original but with its vast and rather solemn entry hall this is a well-meaning hotel, which is very relaxing after a long walk through the small lanes of the gothic quarter or along the 'Ramblas'.

How to get there *(Map 8): facing the cathedral.*

Hotel Gran Vía ★★★

08007 Barcelona
Gran Vía, 642
Tel. (9)3-318 19 00 - Fax (9)3-318 99 97
Sr Garcia

Rooms 53 with air-conditioning, telephone, bath, WC, TV, minibar; elevator. **Price** Single 7,000-8,000Pts, double 10,000-15,500Pts. **Meals** Breakfast 600Pts, served 7:00-11:00. **Restaurant** See pp.201-203. **Credit cards** All major. **Pets** Dogs not allowed. **Facilities** Parking (2,300Pts). **Nearby** Sitges (beach) - Monastery of San Cugat del Valle - Montserrat - Vich; Prat golf course (9 and 18-Hole), San Cugat golf course (18-Hole). **Open** All year.

In the heart of Barcelona, the Hotel Gran Vía has been here since 1936. It was first of all a beautiful private hotel of which a large part of the furniture and original pictures still remain. Without being luxurious, the Gran Vía still has that charm of all cosy establishments and one is rapidly won over by the snug atmosphere reigning here. After an attractive hall, the arcaded gallery and the colonnade of the first floor, one is a little disappointed by the lack of character of the rooms which, even though comfortable, however lack the attraction of the public rooms with their rococo style. The very beautiful dining room is now only used for breakfast, served in summer on the sunny terrace behind the building, while the quieter rooms are also on this side. All in all the welcome is warm.

How to get there *(Map 8): Close to the Paza de Catalunya.*

Hotel San Sebastiàn Playa

08870 Sitges (Barcelona)
Port Alegre, 53
Tel. (9)3-894 86 76 - Fax (9)3-894 04 30
Sra Farina Sharma

Rooms 51 with air-conditioning, telephone, bath, WC, cable TV, video, safe and minibar; elevator. **Price** Single 8,900-13,400Pts, double 13,000-16,900Pts, suite 24,900-26,900Pts. **Meals** Breakfast included, served 7:00-12:00. **Restaurant** "La Concha" Service 13:30-16:00, 20:30-23:00; carte 3,200-6,500Pts. Specialties: Catalan and international cooking. **Credit cards** All major. **Pets** Dogs not allowed. **Facilities** Swimming pool, garage, parking. **Nearby** Monastery of Santes Creus - Monastery Santa Marìa Poblet - Barcelona - Costa Dorada ; Terramar golf course (18-Hole). **Open** All year.

The Hotel San Sebastiàn Playa is relatively new and built in a neo-classical style recalling the architecture of the palaces of the early years of the century. Its site in the seaside resort of Sitges is incomparable at only a hundred meters from the historic center and facing the sea, and it promises its clientele in the front rooms some exceptional morning wakenings. Prices vary with room location. In the reception rooms the decor is modern and uses beautiful and elegant materials. One finds the same sobriety in the rooms, which gives them a rather cold atmosphere, but all are very comfortable. The beach is right close by but the hotel has its own attractive and well sheltered swimming pool. A very good address in this tourist town, very animated in summer, which allows you to alternate calm and distractions.

How to get there (Map 8): 29km south of Barcelona via C246, corniche road along the sea.

Hotel Romàntic

08870 Sitges (Barcelona)
Sant Isidre, 33
Tel. (9)3-894 83 75 - Fax (9)3-894 81 67
Sres Vendrell i Sobrer

Rooms 55 with telephone, bath or shower, WC. **Price** Single 5,100-7,100Pts, double 9,700-9,400Pts, triple 9,700-11,400Pts. **Meals** Breakfast included, served 7:00-11:00. **Restaurant** See pp. 203. **Credit cards** All major. **Pets** Dogs not allowed. **Nearby** Monastery of Santes Creus - Monastery Santa Marìa Poblet - Barcelona - Costa Dorada ; Terramar golf course (18-Hole). **Open** 15. Oct-31. Mar.

This is a charming hotel in a beautiful house in the town of Sitges, some forty kilometers away from the Catalan capital, and very much the fashionable beach. All the hip citizens of Barcelona are to be found here, and the ambiance in summer is exceptional, especially in the evenings at aperitif- and tapas-time, when all the parties start—only to finish in the wee hours of the morning! The rooms are indeed well kept but rather basic and only fitted with showers. On the other hand, the atmosphere is very lively. Painters staying at the hotel have left their frescoes on the walls, while from 6pm onwards one can have a drink, with classical music, at the bar. The shaded garden has many small corners for reading or unwinding in full peace and quiet. The welcome is very friendly and the atmosphere very informal, but the hotel is better suited for bachelors than for family groups.

How to get there (Map 8): 29km south of Barcelona via the C246, the corniche along the sea coast.

Parador Duques de Cardona ★★★★

08261 Cardona (Barcelona)
Castillo de Cardona
Tel. (9)3-869 12 75 - Fax (9)3-869 16 36
Sr Soria Alvarez

Rooms 60 with air-conditioning, telephone, bath, WC, TV, (50 with minibar); elevator. **Price** Double 9,000-12,000Pts, suite 13,780-16,960Pts. **Meals** Breakfast 1,200Pts, served 8:00-11:00; half board + 4,200Pts, full buard + 6,375Pts. **Restaurant** Service 13:30-16:00, 20:30-22:30; menu 3,200Pts, also à la carte. Specialties: Catalan cooking. **Credit cards** All major. **Pets** Dogs not allowed. **Facilities** Parking. **Nearby** in Cardona: Church Sant Vicenç - Salt mountain of Salina. **Open** All year.

Raised by the Dukes of Cardona, this fortress was built at the very beginning of the Middle Ages and modified over the course of the centuries, and for a long time served as a military barracks. Despite its rather impressive proportions, the new occupants have learned how to make the place welcoming: ceilings with caissons and numerous copper-colored carpets all help warm the public rooms. The bedrooms are attractive and well furnished. The view, superb in earler times, is now somwhat compromised as Cardona is one of the major mining towns of the north of the country.

How to get there (Map 8): 97km northwest of Barcelona to Manresa, then C1410.

Gran Hotel Rey don Jaime ★★★★

08860 Castelldefels (Barcelona)
Torre Barona - Avenida del Hotel, 22
Tel. (9)3-665 13 00 - Fax (9)3-665 18 01
Sra Montserrat Pons

Rooms 240 with air-conditioning, telephone, bath, WC, TV and minibar. **Price** Double 14,000-18,000Pts, suite 20,500Pts. **Meals** Breakfast included, served 7:30-10:30; half board + 4,000Pts. **Restaurant** Service 13:30-15:30, 20:30-22:00; menu 3,900Pts. Specialties: arroz negro. **Credit cards** All major. **Pets** Dogs allowed. **Facilities** Indoor swimming pool, tennis, squash, health center, garage, parking. **Nearby** Sitges (beach) - Villafranca del Peredes - Barcelona; Vallomanas golf course (18-hole). **Open** All year.

The Gran Hotel Rey don Jaime is right next to the Barona Tower dating from the 12th century, which, with the chateau, dominated the ancient town of Castrum de Fels, today's Castelldefels. Situated on a small hill, it has a pretty view over the 'gran playa' of Barcelona. The hotel is of very good standing and comfort reigns throughout. Recently restructured, the hotel has been enormously enlarged and the rooms are vast, some with terraces. There is a very shady garden with a pretty swimming pool set at the foot of the tower, all adding to the calm of the site. The proximity to Barcelona makes this an ideal staging post on a Costa Brava that is too overpopulated in the summer.

How to get there *(Map 8): 20km southwest of Barcelona via C245.*

Hotel Llicorella ★★★★

08880 Cubelles (Barcelona)
Carret. C 246 - Camino de San Antonio, 101
Tel. (9)3-895 00 44 - Fax (9)3-895 24 17 - Sra de Adria

Rooms 16 with air-conditioning, telephone, bath, WC, cable TV, safe and minibar. **Price** Single 10,000Pts, double 13,000-19,000Pts, suite 20,000Pts. **Meals** Breakfast 1,100Pts, served 7:00-11:00; half board 15,370Pts, full board 19,540Pts (per pers., 3 days min.). **Restaurant** Service 13:30-16:00, 20:30-23:00; menu 5,680Pts, also à la carte. Specialties: Pimientos del piquillo rellenos de gambas - Higado de pato sobre cebolla y manzana confitadas - Tocinillo de cielo sobre coulis de frambuesa. **Credit cards** All major. **Pets** Dogs not allowed. **Facilities** Parking. **Nearby** Sitges (beach) - Villafranca del Penedes - Barcelona. **Open** All year.

Hardly has one left the many lights of Barcelona than one enters into the heart of Catalonia, where stretches of countryside ever more beautiful than the preceding one follow after each other. In one of these privileged little corners you will find the Hotel Llicorella, a handsome stone residence with a careful recipe of elegance and sobriety. The owner is known to a large number of Catalans as he ran a well-known picture gallery in Barcelona, and has remained in contact with many artists. Still a lover of the arts, he has filled his hotel with many works of recognized artists. All details are aesthetic, while the table does not lack for pretty things and flavors. The rooms, are each dedicated to a different painter, and mix a taste for art with refined comfort. There is also a very good restaurant.

How to get there *(Map 8): 54km southwest of Barcelona via A7, exit Villafranca (No. 29), then C244 and C246.*

Hotel San Bernat ★★★

08460 Montseny (Barcelona)
Tel. (9)3-847 30 11 - Fax (9)3-847 30 11
Sr Pérez Gázquez

Rooms 21 with telephone, bath, WC and TV. **Price** Double 11,725Pts. **Meals** Breakfast included, served 8:00-11:00. **Restaurant** Service 13:30-16:00, 20:30-22:00; menu 2,872Pts, also à la carte. Specialties: Catalan cooking **Credit cards** All major. **Pets** Dogs not allowed. **Facilities** Parking. **Nearby** Sierra of Montseny from San Celoni to Massanet de la Selva, 120 km (Ermitage de Santa Fe, Brull, Tona, Viladrau). **Open** All year.

One gets to the hotel via a small winding and very green-lined lane that climbs up to the high ground of Montseny. The entrance is really attractive: a building covered with ivy, lawns on which the owner's Saint Bernard dogs are playing, and a small pond reflecting the large willow trees. The rooms, small and simple, are pleasant and in good taste, while the bathrooms are ravishing. The quietest rooms face the valley. Do not miss taking your tea on the lawn behind the hotel, to enjoy both the irreplaceable view over the valley and neighboring mountains, and the calm of the spot. The pretty little church is where Saint Bernard halted in earlier days. The San Bernat is the ideal place for a relaxing country stay if no very special reception is expected.

How to get there (Map 8): 70km northeast of Barcelona; or 8km northwest of Montseny, on the road to Tona.

La Reserva ★★★★

Valldoreix - 08190 San Cugat del Vallès(Barcelona)
Ramblas Mossèn Jacint Verdaguer, 41
Tel. (9)3-589 21 21 - Fax (9)3-674 21 00

Rooms 16 with air-conditioning, telephone, bath, WC, TV, safe and minibar; elevator. **Price** Single 18,500-25,000Pts, double 33,000Pts, suite 40,000-73,000Pts. **Meals** Breakfast 1,000Pts, served 7:00-11:30; half board + 4,200Pts. **Restaurant** Service 13:30-16:00, 20:30-22:00; menu 3,000Pts, also à la carte. Specialties: Catalan and international cooking. **Credit cards** All major. **Pets** Dogs not allowed. **Facilities** Garage (15,000Pts). **Nearby** Sitges (beach) - Barcelona - Sierra de Montseny; San Cugat golf course (18-Hole). **Open** All year.

Built in the 1920's on a hill some twenty kilometers away from Barcelona by a wealthy property owner, La Reserva was opened as a hotel for the Olympic Games. This is a unique spot as all the splendor of the house has been preserved. There is a picture collection worthy of a museum, alongside sculptures and bronzes, as well as a remarkable library (with Barcelona as its theme). Lamps, ever-present marble, period furniture and flamboyant carpets all create an opulent atmosphere, which is never in bad taste. The rooms with their vast bathrooms are of course very comfortable, while the 'junior suites' on the upper floor, slightly mansarded and wainscotted, are particularly successful. A terrace descends gently to a flowery garden and the swimming pool, beside which one may also take a meal. In between a museum, a private house and a 'de luxe' hotel, La Reserva certainly deserves a detour.

How to get there *(Map 8): 22km west of Barcelona towards the 'Tibidabo' and the road to the Sant Cugat golf course.*

Parador de Vich ★★★★

08500 Vich (Barcelona)
Tel. (9)3-888 72 11 – Fax (9)3-888 73 11
Sr Martinez

Rooms 36 with air-conditioning, telephone, bath, WC, TV and minibar; elevator. **Price** Single 86,000-100,000Pts, double 10,000-12,000Pts, suite 19,000-23,000Pts. **Meals** Breakfast 1,100Pts, served 8:00-10:30; full board + 6,375Pts (per pers., 2 days min.). **Restaurant** Service 13:30-16:00, 20:30-22:30; menu 3,200Pts, also à la carte. Specialties: Zarzuela de pescado y mariscos, semi-tomba. **Credit cards** All major. **Pets** Dogs not allowed. **Facilities** Swimming pool, tennis, garage, parking. **Nearby** in Vich; Cathedral and Episcopal museum - Costa Dorada - Costa Brava - Barcelona. **Open** All year.

The architecture and decor of this parador are not its major strengths, and the building put up in 1972 under the Franco regime is massive and hardly welcoming. The internal arrangements are not in the best taste. But its greatest quality is its site. For apart from its isolated setting 14 kilometers from Vich, which makes it quiet and restful, it also has the advantage of a magnificent panorama over the Pantana de Sau lake and the Guilleries massif. It is imperative to ask for a front room with a balcony. The swimming pool is very delightful, facing the lake and in the midst of a well-kept garden.

How to get there (Map 8): 69km north of Barcelona via N152; 15km from Vich, towards Roda de Ter.

Hotel Mas Pau ★★★★

17600 Avinyonet de Puigventos - Figueres (Gerona)
Apartado, 135
Tel. (9)72-54 61 54 - Fax (9)72-50 13 77 - Sr T. Gerez

Rooms 7 with air-conditioning, telephone, bath, WC, TV, safe and minibar; elevator. **Price** Double 8,500-12,000Pts, suite 12,000-14,000Pts. **Meals** Breakfast 1,200Pts, served 7:15-10:00. **Restaurant** Service 13:00-16:00, 20:00-23:00; closed Sun night and Mon, in summer closed Mon lunch; carte 4,000-5,500Pts. **Credit cards** All major. **Pets** Dogs not allowed. **Facilities** Swimming pool, parking. **Nearby** in Figueres Museu Dali (Salvador Dali museum) - Cadaqués - Massanet de Cabrenys - Gerona. **Open** All year.

If you decide to stop at Figueres to visit the famous Salvador Dali museum, a detour via Avinyonet is a must. This is where the 'Mas Pau' is to be found, one of the best known gastronomic addresses in the area. A hotel has recently been added, with charm only equalled by its quality. This ancient farm built in the 16th century is right in the country, surrounded by fields. The rooms have been arranged in a new annexe, in the same spirit as the public rooms in the main building. More modern, they also bear witness to the exquisite taste of the owners. It is beautiful, functional and comfortable, with friendly and stylish personnel.

How to get there (Map 9): 58km south of Perpignan; 42km from Gerona via A7, exit Figueres, then take the road to Olot.

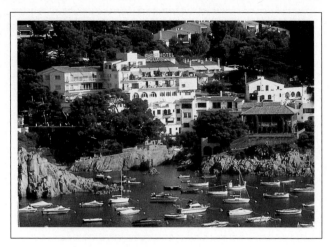

Hotel Aigua Blava ★★★★

Aigua Blava 17255 Begur (Gerona)
Playa de Fornells
Tel. (9)72-62 20 58 – Fax (9)72-62 21 12

Rooms 85 with telephone, bath or shower, WC, TV and minibar. **Price** Single 8,600Pts, double 8,600-15,000Pts, suite 14,000-18,500Pts. **Meals** Breakfast 1,300Pts, served 7:00-11:00; half board + 4,600Pts, full board + 6,000Pts (per per., 3 days min.). **Restaurant** Service 13:30-16:00, 20:30-23:00; menu 3,300Pts, also à la carte. Specialties: Spanish and international cooking. **Credit cards** All major. **Pets** Small dogs allowed. **Facilities** Swimming pool, tennis, volley ball, garage, parking. **Nearby** Pals - Costa Brava - Barcelona - Gerona - Pals golf course (18-Hole). **Open** 1. Mar - 15. Nov.

At the head of a charming creek where rocks covered with pine trees surround the limpid sea, the Aigua Blava enjoys a really beautiful site. It is made up of a group of buildings set around a very attractive small and flowered park. Go for a room with a terrace looking over the sea. With their bright moquette and white walls the rooms are both comfortable and welcoming. As night falls the swimming pool is floodlit and its glow mixes with the lights of the villas all around, thus creating a magic atmosphere. Alas, the cuisine does not live up to the standards of the rest.

How to get there (Map 9): *on the coast north of Barcelona; 46km east of Gerona via A7, exit No. 6.*

Jordi's ★★

17255 Begur (Gerona)
Apartado, 47
Tel. (9)72-30 15 70 - Fax (9)72-61 01 12 - Jordi y Maria

Rooms 8 with bath. **Price** Double 4,750-8,850Pts. **Meals** Breakfast 500Pts, served 8:00-10:00. **Restaurant** Service 13:00-16:00, 20:00-23:00; carte: 3,000Pts. Specialties: Suquet de pescados - Caldereta de langouste - Filete al queso de cabra y bayas de hencero. **Credit cards** Amex, Visa, Eurocard, MasterCard. **Pets** Dogs allowed. **Facilities** Parking. **Nearby** Pals - Costa Brava - Barcelona - Gerona - Pals golf course (18-Hole). **Open** All year (in winter, the week ends only).

This is a very good location well away from the surrounding confusion, and personally run by Jordi. The beautiful house is on the high ground that dominates the surrounding country, and is set among cypresses and pine trees that give a welcoming shade and cool. Eight rooms have been arranged on two levels with very great care; they are beautifully simple, their wood furniture married with cooling floor tiles, their bathrooms impeccable. On the ground floor the rooms all have terraces, but those on the upper floor (the house is built on a slope) have smaller windows. In the restaurant hall around the open fireplace, or on the big terrace protected from the sun, you will feel the original atmosphere of this Catalan house. The cuisine is another strong point with delicious specialties varying with arrivals at the market. The welcome is very friendly.

How to get there *(Map 9): on the coast north of Barcelona; 46km east of Gerona via A7, exit No. 6.*

Chalet del Golf ★★★

17463 Bolvir-Puigcerdà (Gerona)
Tel. (9)72-88 09 62 - Fax (9)72-88 09 66
Sr Lucarini

Rooms 16 with telephone, bath, WC; elevator. **Price** Single 9,000Pts, double 12,000Pts. **Meals** Breakfast 900Pts, served 8:30-11:30; half board + 5,500Pts, full board + 5,900Pts. **Restaurant** Service 13:30-16:00, 20:30-22:30;menu 3,300Pts, also à la carte. **Credit cards** All major. **Pets** Dogs allowed in the rooms. **Facilities** Swimming pool, tennis, golf, squash, parking. **Nearby** Cerdanya Valley - Andorra (a duty free principality) - Bellver de Cerdaña (fishing in the rio Segre) - Skiing (La Molina and Maranges) - Llivia; Cerdaña golf course (18-Hole). **Open** All year except fifteen days before Christmas.

Naturally there is a beautiful golf course while the house that serves as hotel and restaurant is no less charming. Woodlands nearby make timber usage only too easy, and great use is made of it in decorating the hotel, giving it a very warm atmosphere. All the rooms look out over the golf course, and they are simple, but that doesn't matter much—they are mostly used by sports lovers, who spend most of their days outside. In contrast, the management has fitted out a snug restaurant and lounges that make one think of Great Britain. Golf requires this!

How to get there (Map 8): 172km north of Barcelona via N152, then at Puigcerdá via C1313.

Hotel Torre del Remei ★★★★★

17463 Bolvir de Cerdanya (Gerona)
Cami Reial
Tel. (9)72-14 01 82 - Fax (9)72-14 04 49 - Sr Boix

Rooms 8 and 2 suites with air-conditioning, telephone, bath with jacuzzi, WC, cable TV and safe; elevator. **Price** Double 25,000-29,000Pts, suite 37,000-55,000Pts. **Meals** Breakfast 2,200Pts, served 8:00-12:00. **Restaurant** Service 13:00-16:00, 21:00-23:00; carte 6,000Pts. Specialties: Terrina de escalivada y salsa de mostaza - Cola de buey guisada a las siete horas - Medallones de venado marinado con salsa de trufa. **Credit cards** All major. **Pets** Dogs allowed in the rooms. **Facilities** Swimming pool, parking. **Nearby** Cerdanya Valley - Andorra (a duty free principality) - Bellver de Cerdaña (fishing in the rio Segre) - Skiing (La Molina and Maranges) - Llivia; Cerdaña golf course (18-Hole). **Open** All year.

Only fifteen minutes from the border at Bourg-Madame in a superb country of vast prairies and mountains in the real heart of Catalonia, the Hotel Torre del Remei has been installed in a beautiful aristocratic residence dating from the begining of the century. Despite renovation the building has lost nothing of its original character, while the decor is remarkable, allying luxury, charm and comfort. Here are polished floors, crystal lamps and caisson ceilings, alongside contemporary art and furniture with studied lines. One has to salute the restaurant and the personnel, stylish yet efficient, and attentive to your slightest request. Thanks to its exceptional situation, the Torre del Remei, open summer and winter, attracts both sports lovers (close to a golf course and to ski resorts) and lovers of nature and good food.

How to get there *(Map 8): 172km north of Barcelona via N152, then 2km from Puigcerdá via C1313.*

Hotel Balneario Prats ★★★

17455 Caldes de Malavella (Gerona)
Plaça Sant Esteve, 7
Tel. (9)72-47 00 51 - Fax (9)72-47 22 33
Sr Quintana

Rooms 76 with telephone, bath or shower, WC and TV; elevator. **Price** half board for 1 Pers. 7,100-8,400Pts, for 2 pers. 12,400-13,500Pts. **Meals** Breakfast included, served 8:30-10:30. **Restaurant** Service 13:30-14:30, 20:30-21:30; menu 2,500Pts, also à la carte. Specialties: Catalan and international cooking **Credit cards** All major. **Pets** Small dogs allowed. **Facilities** Thermal swimming pool, Sauna (4,000Pts), health center, parking. **Nearby** Thermal station - Gerona. **Open** All year.

A strong scent of pines tickles the nostrils.... It comes from the garden and terrace with their trees. It is in this way that one approaches the Hotel Balneario Prats. One sees an archway full of charm and a few remnants saved from the last century, and also from the 1930s. The hotel has been subject to several transformations and, as a result, some rooms are modern and others not. Try to reserve a room 'in the old style'—and number 147 in particular: it has preserved its Art-Deco furniture and also enjoys a very pretty view.

How to get there *(Map 9): 83km northeast of Barcelona; 22km south of Gerona via N2; at km 17 take the small road to the left.*

Hotel Balneario Vichy Catalan ★★★

17455 Caldes de Malavella (Gerona)
Avenida Dr Furest, 32
Tel. (9)72-47 00 00 - Fax (9)72-47 00 00
Srs Delemus Tarres

Rooms 86 with telephone, bath or shower, WC (65 with telephone); elevator. **Price** half board for 1 Pers. 7,100-8,400Pts, for 2 pers. 12,400-13,500Pts. **Meals** Breakfast included, served 8:30-10:30. **Restaurant** with air-conditioning; Service 13:30-14:30, 20:30-21:30; menu 2,500Pts, also à la carte. Specialties: Catalan and international cooking **Credit cards** All major. **Pets** Small dogs allowed. **Facilities** Indoor swimming pool, tennis (600Pts), health center, parking. **Nearby** Thermal station - Gerona. **Open** All year.

A spa just as one imagines it.... Built at the end of the last century with stone columns, park and fountain, and a tiled floor in the old style. As for the thermal baths, they are modern. The rooms are very much less so, even if they have all been renovated; opt for those overlooking the park. The bar has conserved its vaulting and beams, but above all its cool. It gives onto an adorable small Moorish patio, flanked by its tiny chapel in a typical turn-of-the-century style.

How to get there (Map 9): 83km northeast of Barcelona; 22km south of Gerona via N2; at km 17 take the small road to the left.

Hotel Edelweiss ★★★

17867 Camprodón (Gerona)
Carret. de Sant Joan, 28
Tel. (9)72-74 09 13 - Fax (9)72-74 07 04
Sr Rous

Rooms 21 with telephone, bath, WC and TV; elevator. **Price** Double 10,000Pts.
Meals Breakfast 700-1,300Pts, served 8:00-10:30; half board + 4,200Pts.
No Restaurant. Credit cards All major. **Pets** Dogs allowed. **Facilities** Parking.
Nearby in Camprodón: Church of San Pedro - Beget (San Cristófol Church and
the bell tower) - Llanars (San Esteve Church) - Molló (Santa Cecilia Church) -
Ripoll (Santa Marìa Church) - Setcases; Camprodón golf course (18-Hole).
Open All year except Christmas.

The facade is already welcoming and one step inside you
immediately notice the refinement of the place. The owner
claims he decorated his hotel just as if it was his own home.
The pieces of furniture are only copies but they are so neat !
Not one fault can be found with them. The bathrooms are
harmonious. In the dining room, only breakfasts are
served—but what breakfast! A sideboard recalls those of our
grandmothers, with their large pots of home-made jams, onto
which bright labels have been stuck to make them more chic. A
warm welcome and plenty of attention mean you will certainly
want to keep the hotel's card close at hand.

How to get there *(Map 9): 133km north of Barcelona via N152 to
Ripoll, then C151.*

La Mère Michelle

17121 Corça (Gerona)
Calle Mayor, 11
Tel. (9)72-63 05 35 - Fax (9)72-63 05 35
Sra Michelle Amram

Rooms 3 with bath and WC. **Price** Double 9,000Pts. **Meals** Breakfast 900Pts, served 8:00-13:00; half board + 3,500Pts, full board + 6,000Pts. **Restaurant** Service 12:30-16:30, 20:30-23:30; menu 2,500-3,000Pts. Specialties: French cooking. **Credit cards** Visa, Eurocard, MasterCard. **Pets** Small dogs allowed. **Nearby** Gerona - Figueres (Salvador Dali Museum); 10 golf courses. **Open** July, Aug, Sept and all week ends and holidays out of season. Except in Feb.

Close to Gerona everybody knows the small restaurant La Mère Michelle, opened by a French woman living in Spain. The small village of Corça is very well sited for holidays, just a few kilometers away from the regional capital of Gerona, at about twenty kilometers from the beaches and surrounded by golf courses. All the conviviality of a family home has been retained: beams and old furniture give a lot of warmth to the decor. It is the same in the restaurant, very small, where one has to rush to reserve if you wish to try the good French specialties of the house: scents of Mediterranean cuisine but also all the generosity of the cooking of Alsace. Three rooms have recently been opened, prettily decorated and comfortable, but more in the spirit of a boarding house than a traditional hotel (no TV, no direct phone but on the other hand, a small fridge in each room along with tea- and coffee-making facilities and room service). This is a non-typical address for Spain.

How to get there (Map 9): *30km from Gerona via E15 exit Gerona North, then towards La Bisbal.*

Hotel Grévol ★★★★

17869 Llanars (Gerona)
Carretera de Camprodòn
Tel. (9)72-74 10 13 - Fax (9)72-74 10 87 - Sr Sole

Rooms 36 with telephone, bath or shower, WC, TV, and minibar; elevator. **Price** Double 13,900-17,300Pts. **Meals** Breakfast 1,100Pts (buffet), served 8:00-10:00; full board + 6,800Pts (per pers., 3 days min.). **Restaurant** Service 13:00-15:30, 21:00-22:30; closed Mon, May and Nov; menu 3,500Pts, also à la carte. Specialties: regional cooking. **Credit cards** Amex, Visa, Eurocard, MasterCard. **Pets** Dogs not allowed. **Facilities** Indoor swimming pool, minigolf, parking. **Nearby** in Llanars: San Esteve Church - Camprodón (Church of San Pedro) - Beget (San Cristófol Church and the bell tower) - Molló (Santa Cecilia Church) - Ripoll (Santa Marìa Church) - Setcases; Camprodón golf course (18-Hole). **Open** All year.

The recently built and very well-equipped Grévol recalls those large Austrian chalet-hotels. The Camprodòn region attracts a family clientele wanting to get some fresh air in the refreshing setting of the Pyrenees, and to do engage in an open-air sport such as golf, skiing or horseback riding. The hotel rooms are charming with panelled walls, furniture in wood and oak in Tyrolian style, which is also found in the main room of the restaurant around an open fireplace. All this creates a very comfortable atmosphere. With a more than complete games room/hall (bowling, table football, billiards, etc.), children will be more than happy. After a day's hiking the family can then swim in the covered pool or unwind in the huge jacuzzi.

How to get there (Map 8): *129km north of Barcelona via N152 to Ripoll, then C151. At 3km on the road from Camprodòn to Setcases.*

Hotel Santa Marta ★★★★

17310 Lloret de Mar (Gerona)
Playa de Santa Cristina
Tel. (9)72-36 49 04 – Fax (9)72-36 92 80
Sr Noguera

Rooms 78 with air-conditioning, telephone, bath, WC, cable TV and minibar; elevator. **Price** Single 11,000-17,000Pts, double 16,000-31,000Pts, suite 25,000-44,000Pts. **Meals** Breakfast 1,650Pts, served 8:00-11:00; half board + 7,425Pts, full board + 10,500Pts (per pers.). **Restaurant** Service 13:30-15:30, 20:30-22:30; menu 5,775Pts, also à la carte. Specialties: Rollitos de salmon con cangrejos - Suquet de mero. **Credit cards** All major. **Pets** Dogs allowed in the rooms (+ 800 Pts). **Facilities** Swimming pool, tennis (1,000Pts), beach, parking. **Nearby** Costa Brava - Road from Lloret del Mar to Tossa del Mar; Gerona. **Open** 1. Mar - 15. Dec.

This was the most fashionable hotel on the Costa Brava thirty years ago. It is certainly modern, and with an exceptional situation that is unique in the region. It is lost in woodland, with a facade clinging to the rocks and facing the sea. There is also a fully equipped private beach, and all this in such divine peace and quiet. The rooms are classical, but perhaps too much so !

How to get there (Map 9): 39km south of Gerona via A7, exit No. 9; 3km from Lloret.

Cal Borrell ★★

17539 Meranges (Gerona)
Regreso, 3
Tel. (9)72-88 00 33 - Fax (9)72-88 01 44
Sr Forn

Rooms 8 with telephone, bath and WC. **Price** Double 8,000Pts. **Meals** Breakfast 350-800Pts, served 9:00-11:00; half board + 3,500Pts, full board + 6,000Pts. **Restaurant** Service 13:00-17:00, 21:00-23:00; carte 3,000-4,500Pts. Specialties: Pork, game. **Credit cards** Visa, Eurocard, MasterCard. **Pets** Dogs not allowed. **Facilities** Parking. **Nearby** Cerdanya Valley - Andorra (a duty free principality) - Bellver de Cerdaña (fishing in the rio Segre) - Skiing (La Molina and Maranges) - Llivia; Cerdaña golf course (18-Hole). **Open** 1. Apr - 31. Dec and the week ends all the year.

Cal Borrell is a former farmhouse refurbished and transformed into a hotel in the heart of a picture-perfect mountain village. The rooms have magnificent wooden ceilings and beams, and all have a view over the valley. Try to get the room called 'The house on the prairie', with its mezzanine and superb panorama. There is a guaranteed warm mountain atmosphere, perfect for relaxing and rest. One also appreciates the good cuisine served in the restaurant as the Cal Borrell is known for its excellent table.

How to get there (Map 8): 191km north of Barcelona via N152 to Puigcerdá, then C1313 for about 7km; take the small road to the right.

Hotel Carles Camós Big-Rock ★★★★

17250 Playa de Aro (Gerona)
Barri de Fanals, 5
Tel. (9)72-81 80 12 - Fax (9)72-81 89 71
Sr Camós

Rooms 5 suites with air-conditioning, telephone, bath, WC, TV, and minibar.
Price Suite 16,000-24,000Pts. **Meals** Breakfast 1,150Pts, served 8:30-11:00.
Restaurant Service 13:00-15:30, 20:30-22:30; carte 3,600-4,800Pts.
Specialties: Lomo de merluza con patatitas - Suquet de rape y langostinos -
Capriccio de crema con fresitas. **Credit cards** All major. **Pets** Dogs allowed.
Facilities Swimming pool, parking. **Nearby** Gerona - Costa Brava; Costa Brava
golf course (18-Hole). **Open** 1. Feb - 31. Dec, closed Mon and Sun night in
winter.

Known first for its restaurant, Big-Rock also has a few
rooms. Isolated in the country, this is a large and ancient
building refurbished with taste in the last century. The owner is
an excellent chef and great personality, as he founded the
'Brotherhood of Happy Joy', and everything with him is
genuine and simply breathes fun. The flowered terraces glory in
the sun while the furniture smells sweetly of polished wood.
The rooms are in fact all suites, and deserve a special mention
for their luxurious amenities. Tasteful pictures decorate the
walls, so why be surprised if the King of Spain himself
sometimes passes by here ?

How to get there (Map 9): 37km southeast of Gerona via C250.

El Moli ★★

17706 Pont de Molins (Gerona)
Carret. las Escaules
Tel. (9)72-52 80 11 - Fax (9)72-52 81 01
Sr Llado Grau

Rooms 8 with telephone, bath and WC. **Price** Double 8,000Pts. **Meals** Breakfast 600Pts, served 7:30-10:00. **Restaurant** Service 13:15-15:30, 19:30-22:30; carte 1,800-2,800Pts. Specialties: Regional cooking. **Credit cards** All major. **Pets** Dogs allowed in the restaurant. **Facilities** Tennis (800Pts), parking. **Nearby** Figueres(Salvador Dali museum) - Cadaqués - Gerona - Massaner de Cabrenys. **Open** Holy Week - Oct.

S et back from a country road stands a former 18th-century mill, restored and converted into a hotel-restaurant some ten years ago. Here it is clear that someone loves secondhand things: the mill stones now serve as low tables; all the sideboards, cupboards, troughs and beds were bought from local antique dealers. Five meters in front of the hotel terrace flows the River Monje, lined with magnificent trees. The restaurant has a good reputation and attracts a French clientele, as the frontier is only some twenty kilometers away. The rooms are charming, while No. 102 is the largest and overlooks the river. Taking count of the very reasonable prices as well, 'El Moli' certainly merits a detour.

How to get there (Map 9): 43km north of Gerona via A7, exit No. 3.

Hostal de la Gavina ★★★★

17248 S' Agaró (Gerona)
Plaza de la Rosaleda
Tel. (9)72-32 11 00 - Fax (9)72-32 15 73
Sra Requena

Rooms 74 with air-conditioning, telephone, bath, WC, TV, video, safe and minibar; elevator. **Price** Double 21,000-38,000Pts, suite 29,000-45,000Pts. **Meals** Breakfast 1,950Pts, served 7:30-11:30; half board + 7,450Pts, + 10,600Pts (per pers.). **Restaurant** Service 13:00-15:30, 20:30-23:30; menu 5,500Pts. Specialties: Fish. **Credit cards** All major. **Pets** Dogs not allowed. **Facilities** Swimming pool, sauna, paddle-tennis, parking. **Nearby** Gerona - Costa Brava; Costa Brava golf course (18-Hole). **Open** Holy Week - 20. Oct.

This is an old house that the owners transformed little by little into a hotel and then a hotel 'de luxe'. It enjoys an enviable situation: all rooms, the flowery terrace and the patio have a superb view over the sea. The rooms are also all different and personalized. If you have the means, go for the royal suite, but you have to pay out in the Louis XV style as well !

How to get there (Map 9): 34km southeast of Gerona via C250.

C A T A L U N Y A

Balneario Termas Orión ★★

17404 Santa Colomá de Farnés (Gerona)
Tel. (9)72-84 00 65 - Fax (9)72-84 04 66
Sr Campeny

Rooms 60 with telephone, bath or shower, WC (40 with TV); elevator. **Price** Full board 6,000-9,000Pts. **Meals** Breakfast included, served 8:30-10:00. **Restaurant** With air-conditioning. Service 13:30-15:00, 20:30-22:00; menu 2,100Pts, also à la carte. Specialties: Catalan cooking. **Credit cards** Visa, Eurocard, MasterCard. **Pets** Dogs not allowed. **Facilities** Indoor swimming pool, tennis (700Pts), parking. **Nearby** Thermal station - Gerona. **Open** 15. Feb - 15. Jan.

On leaving the village and at the end of an alley of huge trees, you come upon this gleaming while building with stone columns. Built in the last century, the hotel has kept all its allure and atmosphere: everything here has the atmosphere times past. A gramophone, a magic lantern, a collection of old spectacles, all seem to have always been here. There is even a lounge-theater (the former owner was a great actress). The natural springs have been completely refurbished in recent times, and only the mosaics of the earlier swimming pool remain; the former marble baths serve as flower pots. The rooms are simple and the bathrooms have an unmatched comfort. Choose the newer rooms or those looking out on the vast stone terrace on the park. It is all very romantic.

How to get there (Map 9): 23km southwest of Gerona, and 2km from Santa Colomá.

Hotel Mas Torrellas *

17246 Santa Cristina de Aró (Gerona)
Carret. Santa Cristina a Playa de Aro, km 1,713
Tel. (9)72-83 75 26 - Fax. (9)72-83 75 27
Famille Carrera

Rooms 17 with telephone, bath, WC, TV and minibar. **Price** Double 6,000-11,000Pts. **Meals** Breakfast included, served 8:00-11:00; half board + 2,000Pts, full board + 4,000Pts. **Restaurant** Service 13:00-16:00, 19:30-23:30; menu 2,000Pts, also à la carte. Specialties: Pastel de esparragos - Zarzuela - Capricho de la casa. **Credit cards** All major. **Pets** Dogs not allowed. **Facilities** Swimming pool, tennis, sauna, parking. **Nearby** Gerona - Costa Brava - Costa Brava golf course (18-Hole). **Open** All year.

A real discovery... A few years ago the owners spotted and bought a residence in the midst of ten hectares of land, then restored it and fitted it out as a hotel. It is not luxurious: they have opted for personality and ambiance. The famous Catalan vaultings are everywhere, above all in the former stables now converted into the dining room. A mention for the cellar-bar with its original old beams and wine barrels from all regions of the country! The rooms are neat—the best is choose No. 18, which looks out on the countryside and mountain, and was a round bath. For the moment this hotel has only a one-star rating but, given all the advantages on offer, profit from this quickly before its prices rise to those of a three-star.

How to get there (Map 9): 31km southeast of Gerona via C250.

Mas de Torrent ★★★★★

17123 Torrent (Gerona)
Tel. (9)72-30 32 92 - Fax (9)72-30 32 93
Sr Berenjui

Rooms 30 with air-conditionning, telephone, bath, WC, cable TV, safe and minibar. **Price** Double 25,000-30,000Pts, suite 28,000-35,000Pts. **Meals** Breakfast 1,850Pts, served 8:00-10:00; half board + 5,800Pts, full board + 9,300Pts. **Restaurant** Service 13:30-15:00, 20:30-23:30; menus 3,500-6,000Pts, also à la carte. Specialties: regional and international cooking. **Credit cards** All major. **Pets** Dogs allowed in the rooms (1,750Pts). **Facilities** Swimming pool, tennis, parking. **Nearby** Gerona - Costa Brava - Costa Brava golf course (18-Hole), Pals golf course (18-Hole). **Open** All year.

In the heart of Catalonia, nine kilometers from the most fashionable beaches of the Costa Brava (Aigua Blava, Bégur, etc.), a large 18th-century farm building, now completely restored, has been offering its cuisine and suites for some years. The appeal is to a clientele sensitive to comfort and gentle manners. Everything has been arranged in exquisite taste; all the rooms are different and decorated with a lot of finesse. Twenty bungalows have been built for families in a private garden. The restaurant is delightful and one should note a collection of prints in the dining room in honor of Picasso. The ambiance is very calm and relaxed. What more could one want?

How to get there (Map 9): 36km east of Gerona via A7, exit No. 6, towards Torrent.

Hotel Caldas ★

25528 Caldas de Bohi (Lérida)
Tel. (9)73-69 62 30 – Fax (9)73-69 60 30
Sr Moriscot Pidemunt

Rooms 104 (31 with bath and WC). **Price** Double 38,000-95,000Pts. **Meals** Breakfast 530Pts, served 8:00-10:30; half board + 2,600Pts, full board + 3,980Pts (per pers.). **Restaurant** Service 14:00-15:30, 21:00-22:00; menu 2,100Pts, also à la carte. Specialties: Truchas de la casa - Carn dolla. **Credit cards** not accepted. **Pets** Dogs not allowed. **Facilities** Thermal swimming pool, tennis (1,000Pts), sauna (1,000Pts), garage (500Pts). **Nearby** Bohí Valley from Pont de Suert to Caldes de Bohi (Romanesque churches of Durro, Erill-Aval, Sant Climent de Taùll, Santa Maria) - Excursions in the Aigües Tortes National Park (San Maurici lake) and in the Vall d'Aran. **Open** 25 June - 30. Sept.

The green and winding mountain road ends at a group of hotels at an altitude of 1,500 meters. It was on this site more than sixty years ago that the most important thermal spa in Spain opened. A rare environment and divine peace surround this complex of hotels with its 37 natural springs. A remarkably equiped sporting complex naturally makes this site even more attractive. Our choice has fallen on the very smallest hotel in the complex, which is full of charm. There is a terrace with climbing plants to welcome you both an adorable patio, attractive little corners. The ceilings of all the rooms retain their ancient beams. But make no mistake about it: the whole place is simple, like the people running it, and the prices as well....

How to get there *(Map 7): 145km north of Lérida via N230; 3km after the Suert bridge, take small road to the right.*

Hotel El Castell ★★★★

25700 La Seu d'Urgell (Lérida)
Carret N 60
Tel. (9)73-35 07 04 - Fax (9)73-35 15 74
Sr Jaume Tápies Travé - Sr Jaume Tàpies Ibern

Rooms 37 and 1 suite with air-conditioning, telephone, bath, WC, cable TV, safe and minibar. **Price** Single 11,000Pts, double 15,500Pts, suite 25,000Pts. **Meals** Breakfast 1,500Pts, served 7:30-10:30; half board + 4,200Pts. **Restaurant** Service 13:00-15:30, 20:00-22:30; carte 4,200-6,800Pts. Specialties: Raviolis de cigalas con mousse de calabacin - Risotto de bogavente con moixernons y trufa. **Credit cards** All major. **Pets** Dogs allowed in the rooms. **Facilities** Swimming pool, parking. **Nearby** in Seu: Santa Marìa Cathedral - Monastery Sant Serni de Tavérnoles in Anserall - Castellciutat - Excursions into the Vall d'Aran - The Cerdanya: Bellver de Cerdanya, Llivia, Puigcerdà - Andorra (Duty Free Principality). **Open** 15. Feb - 15. Jan.

It is on the summit of a gently sloping hill, at the foot of which lies the medieval town of Seo d'Urgel, that El Castell is to be found. In this hotel protected by its mountain (the Sierra del Cadí), everything is organized to profit from such a privileged site. A remarkable comfort characterizes the place with the ground floor rooms enjoying a terrace or private garden, while those on the upper floor have just been renovated. In addition, all enjoy a personalized decor. The restaurant is gastronomic. Truly a hotel for those insisting on style, nature and good living.

How to get there (Map 8): 133km northeast of Lérida via C1313.

Parador Castillo de la Zuda ★★★★

43500 Tortosa (Tarragona)
Castillo de la Zuda
Tel. (9)77-44 44 50 – Fax (9)77-44 44 58
Sr Esteban

Rooms 82 with air-conditioning, telephone, bath, WC, TV and minibar. **Price** Double 9,500-13,000Pts. **Meals** Breakfast 1,200Pts, served 8:00-10:30; half board + 4,200Pts, full board + 6,475Pts (per pers. 2 days min.). **Restaurant** Service 13:30-14:30, 20:00-22:15; menu 3,200Pts. Specialties: regional cooking. **Credit cards** All major. **Pets** Dogs not allowed. **Facilities** Swimming pool, parking. **Nearby** in Tortosa: Cathedral - Morella - Hunting and fishing in the Ebro Delta. **Open** All year.

The château of La Zuda takes its name from the well which according to Arab sources was sunk within the walls in the year 944, and which can still be seen today. This ancient Roman town has had a tumultuous history, becoming in turn a Arab fortress, a prison in the 12th century, and then a royal residence before being ceded to the Templars. Inside the dining room has kept four huge windows and three open fireplaces as witnesses of such a past. The rooms have terraces with a magnificent panorama. But it is from the swimming pool that one has the best view over Tortosa and the fertile valley of the Ebro, all with a backdrop of the mountains of Tortosa and Beceite, a huge hunting reserve.

How to get there *(Map 16): 83km southwest of Tarragona via A7.*

Parador Via de la Plata ★★★★

06800 Mérida (Badajoz)
Plaza de la Constitución, 3
Tel. (9)24-31 38 00 - Fax (9)24-31 92 08
Sr Morales Laveria

Rooms 82 with air-conditioning, telephone, bath, WC, TV and minibar; elevator. **Price** Double 16,000Pts. **Meals** Breakfast 1,200Pts, served 7:30-11:00; full board + 6,970Pts (per pers. 2 days min.). **Restaurant** Service 13:00-16:00, 20:30-22:30; menu 3,500Pts, also à la carte. Specialties: Gazpacho extremeno - Pastel del convento. **Credit cards** All major. **Pets** Dogs not allowed. **Facilities** garage (500Pts), parking. **Nearby** Roman Mérida: Roman Art Museum, Roman Theater, Roman Amphitheater, Roman bridge - Montijo - Embalse de Proserpina - Medelin. **Open** All year.

Mérida is a major tourist center where one comes to see the numerous Roman, Visigoth and Arab remains, and the parador is installed in an ancient convent, itself built on the ruins of a Roman temple. It has known diverse fortunes, even having been a prison! But have no fear, no traces remain of this former ocupation. Two huge lounges, one in the former chapel, a dining room and some very beautiful rooms have been fitted out around the ever traditional interior courtyard. There is also a delightful garden decorated with the Roman sculptures brought to light during the building work.

How to get there (Map 17): 68km south of Cáceres via N630.

Hotel Emperatriz ★★★

06800 Mérida (Badajoz)
Plaza de España, 19
Tel. (9)24-31 31 11 - Fax (9)24-30 03 76
Sr Simancas

Rooms 42 with air-conditioning, telephone, bath, WC, and TV. **Price** Single 5,300-6,000Pts, double 9,700-10,970Pts, suite 10,350-11,700Pts. **Meals** Breakfast 600Pts, served 8:00-11:00; half board + 2,100Pts, full board + 3,600Pts (per pers. 3 days min.). **Restaurant** Service 13:30-16:00, 20:30-23:00; menu 1,500Pts, also à la carte. Specialties: Carne a la brasa - Caldereta de cordero.**Credit cards** Amex, Visa, Eurocard, MasterCard. **Pets** Dogs allowed in the rooms. **Facilities** garage (500Pts), parking. **Nearby** Roman Mérida: Roman Art Museum, Roman Theater, Roman Amphitheater, Roman bridge - Montijo - Embalse de Proserpina - Medelin. **Open** All year.

Built at the end of the 16th century, this former palace has offered hospitality to numerous crowned heads throughout its history. The interior is arranged around a large covered patio. As the rooms are being fully refurbished, ask for one of the most recent ones, spacious with their pretty bathrooms, while the nicest ones look onto the main square, which is happily animated. Some rooms have small balconies. The Emperatriz is not a 'grand luxe' hotel but rather a comfortable establishment with affordable prices. You will appreciate the Talavera tilework marrying so well with the stone of the walls, and the basement-bar in the former cellars. This is the place to stopover at if you wish to visit the famous Roman ruins of Mérida, or just it you are en route towards Andalusia.

How to get there (Map 17): 68km south of Cáceres via N630.

Hotel Melià Càceres ★★★★

10003 Càceres
Plaza de San Juan, 11
Tel. (9)27-21 58 00 - Fax (9)27-21 40 70

Rooms 85 with air-conditioning, telephone, bath, WC, cable TV, safe and minibar; elevator. **Price** Single 12,400Pts, double 15,500Pts, suite 19,850Pts. **Meals** Breakfast 1,275Pts (buffet), served 7:30-11:00; full board + 6,375Pts (per pers.). **Restaurant** "La Indias" Service 13:00-16:00, 20:30-23:00; menu 3,500Pts, also à la carte. Specialties: regional cooking. **Credit cards** All major. **Pets** Dogs not allowed. **Nearby** in Càceres: Barrio Monumental, Plaza de Santa Maria, Palacio de los Golfines de Abajo; Sanctuario de la Virgen de la Montaña - Arroyo de la Luz. **Open** All year.

A superb town and admirably preserved, the old town ('Barrio Monumental') of Càceres is a real museum of Spanish gothic town architecture. The Melià Càceres is in a former palace of the aristocratic Ovendo family, which distinguished itself in America and had a number of such palaces built. All the original structure has been preserved and one enters by a heavy wooden door opening on to the Plaza de San Juan. A large central patio allows a soft light to enter the hall giving access to the reception rooms. Seating and tables have been arranged around some ancient wells to better exploit the serene atmosphere. The bar has been installed in the former stables, covered with magnificent brick vaulting. The rooms are decorated with taste and we recommend those giving onto the square shaded by its bay trees and palms. Comfort is very good and the breakfasts delicious, while the restaurant is also much appreciated. A very good hotel where one is received by a competent and delightful staff.

How to get there (Map 17): 300 km west of Madrid.

Hospederia del Real Monasterio ★★

10140 Guadalupe (Cáceres)
Plaza Juan Carlos I
Tel. (9)27-36 70 00 - Fax (9)27-36 71 77
Sr Simancas

Rooms 47 with air-conditioning, telephone, bath, WC and TV; elevator. **Price** Single: 4,700Pts, double 6,900Pts, suite 15,750Pts. **Meals** Breakfast 750Pts, served 8:30-10:30, full board + 4,390Pts (per pers. 2 days min.). **Restaurant** Service 13:30-15:30, 21:00-22:30, menu 2,350Pts, also à la carte. Specialties: Migas extremeñas - Cabrito asado - Sopa de tomate. **Credit cards** Visa, Eurocard, MasterCard. **Pets** Dogs not allowed. **Facilities** Parking. **Nearby** Monastery of Guadalupe - Ermitage de Humilladero - Caramero - Logrosán. **Open** 12. Feb - 12. Jan.

An impressive and grandiose ensemble, both warrior and monastic, this monastery was an important cultural center, and the Franciscan Community occupying it today has chosen to open a hotel in one part of the monastery. From the hallway one has a very beautiful view on one of the most enchanting corners of the edifice, 'Los Caídos'. Lounges, a dining room and large rooms are spread around the cloister, a small Gothic masterpiece, which is covered with a canopy in summer. Naturally you should visit the monastery with its facade on the town square, and the 'mudejar' cloister and church that has conserved an impressive collection of works of art, including several exceptional pictures by Zurbarán in the sacristy.

How to get there (Map 18): 139km east of Cáceres via N521, then C524 and C401.

Parador Zurbarán ★★★

10140 Guadalupe (Cáceres)
Marqués de la Romana, 12
Tel. (9)27-36 70 75 - Fax (9)27-36 70 76 - Sr Arias

Rooms 40 with telephone, bath, WC, TV, minibar; elevator. **Price** Double 16,900Pts, suite 25,000-9,000-11,500Pts. **Meals** Breakfast 1,100Pts served 8:00-10:30, full board + 6,375Pts (per pers., 2 days min.). **Restaurant** Service 13:00-16:00, 20:30-22:30; menu 3,200Pts, also à la carte. Specialties: Cabrito asado - Sopa de arroz cacereña - Bacalao monacal - Caldereta de Cordero. **Credit cards** All major. **Pets** Dogs allowed. **Facilities** Parking (1,700Pts). **Nearby** Monastery of Guadalupe - Ermitage de Humilladero - Caramero - Logrosán. **Open** All year.

Guadalupe was an important center of pilgrimage and today the grandiose monastery, the Zurbarán and the museum (with a very beautiful collection of lace, among others), all merit a stop here. The ancient St. John the Baptist hospital from the 18th century now houses the hotel. It certainly does not have the prestige of the monastery but its interior layout has a lot more charm. The lounges and dining room are once again arranged around the patio, whose arcades are invaded by orange trees, and in the summer one lunches in the shade of the gallery. The rooms are very prettily decorated but it is preferable to ask for those in the new building, which have a view over the mountains, village and the incredible monastery situated right in front. On the rear side is the swimming pool in the midst of a very flowery garden, and much appreciated in the summer.

How to get there (Map 18): 139km east of Cáceres via N521, then C524 and C401.

Parador Carlos V ★★★

10450 Jarandilla de la Vera (Cáceres)
Tel. (9)27-56 01 17 - Fax (9)27-56 00 88
Sr Fagesa

Rooms 56 with air-conditioning, telephone, bath, WC, TV and minibar. **Price** Double 12,500Pts. **Meals** Breakfast 1,200Pts served 8:00-11:00, full board + 6,375Pts (per pers.). **Restaurant** Service 13:00-16:30, 20:30-22:30; menu 3,200Pts, also à la carte. Specialties: Cabrito - Calderetas de Cordero. **Credit cards** All major. **Pets** Dogs not allowed. **Facilities** Swimming pool, tennis, parking. **Nearby** Cuacos de Yuste and Monastery of Yuste - Garganta la Olla - Cathédrale de Plasencia. **Open** All year.

In the north of Extremadura in the wild country of the Vera, this 14th- and 15th-century chateau is to be found. The very well-preserved edifice still has its beautiful surrounding wall, elegant angle towers and a drawbridge. The building is built around a flowered patio, and one facade consists of two arcaded galleries and a stone balcony worked in the oriental style. It is here that Charles V lodged before retiring to the Yuste monastery. The dining room occupies the ground floor while on the upper floor the lounge opens onto a balcony dominating the patio. The furniture is simple but the caisson ceilings, size of the rooms, lamps, medallions and trophees, all contribute to the chateau spirit. The rooms are both perfect and comfortable.

How to get there (Map 11): 141km northeast of Cáceres via N630 to Plasencia, then C501.

E X T R E M A D U R A

Parador de Trujillo ★★★★

23003 Trujillo (Cáceres)
Plaza de Santa Clara
Tel. (9)27-32 13 50 - Fax (9)27-32 13 66
Sr Ricos

Rooms 46 with telephone, bath, WC, TV and minibar. **Price** Double 12,500-13,000Pts. **Meals** Breakfast 1,200Pts served 8:00-11:00, full board + 6,375Pts (per pers.). **Restaurant** Service 13:00-16:30, 21:00-23:00; menu 3,200Pts, also à la carte. Specialties: Tenca, cordero asado. **Credit cards** All major. **Pets** Dogs not allowed. **Facilities** Swimming pool, tennis, parking. **Nearby** in Trujillo: Plaza Mayor and church of Santa Maria la Mayor - Santa Cruz de la Sierra - Càceres - Guadalupe - National Park of Monfrague. **Open** All year.

Trujillo was the home base of the Conquistadors, as recalled by the equestrian statue of F. Pizarro on the main square, and it is a beautiful town with a host of medieval and Renaissance monuments. The parador is in the ancient convent founded in the 16th century by order of the Immaculate Conception. Built around a courtyard, the cloister is planted with orange trees and has three facades in Renaissance style, with arcatures topped by a gallery with Tuscan small columns. The interior decoration is rather impersonal, particularly in the rooms which, however, lack for no comfort. Some have terraces entirely covered with a trellis, the traditional manner in this region of protecting against the heat. The hotel is air-conditioned and has a swimming pool.

How to get there *(Map 18): 47km east of Cáceres via N521; the parador is located in the lower part of town.*

155

Posada Finca de Santa Marta

Pago de San Clemente
23003 Herguijuela-Trujillo (Cáceres)
Tél. (9)27 31 92 03
Sr Helink - Sra Rodriguez-Gimeno

Rooms 8 with bath. **Price** Double 8,000-10,000Pts. **Meals** Breakfast included served 8:00-10:00, half board 6,500Pts (per pers.). **Restaurant** Evening meals; menu 2,500Pts. Specialties: regional cooking. **Credit cards** All major. **Pets** Dogs allowed. **Facilities** Swimming pool, parking. **Nearby** in Trujillo: Plaza Mayor and church of Santa Maria la Mayor - Santa Cruz de la Sierra - Càceres - Guadalupe - National Park of Monfrague. **Open** All year.

On the National V road linking Madrid and Lisbon, Trujillo is a good staging post where one can visit its 'Plaza Mayor', famous for its arcades and renaissance Palace. One can try the tomato soup with figs, and its braised pork ('la morada'), while - even better - one can now stay in the countryside at the Finca de Santa Marta, a rare 'cortijò' converted for 'green tourism'. This farm-manor house, known in the region as a 'lagar' - where oil and wine are produced - offers eight beautiful rooms. A long and rigorous restoration has preserved all the authenticity of the buildings: one can still visit the mill, converted into a vast lounge-dining room, winepress, cellars and stables, sheepfolds and even the little chapel. The rooms have been subjected to all the care of the owner-decorator and have very refined decors: old wood and tiles have been restored to mix in harmony with the regional furniture and the most up-to-date comfort facilities. The garden is delightful, planted with olive, cherry and almond trees, all offering beautiful spring days in white and pink.

How to get there *(Map 18): 50km east of Càceres via N521 to Trujillo, then 14km towards Guadalupe via C524 .*

Hotel de Los Reyes Católicos ★★★★★

15705 Santiago de Compostela (La Coruña)
Plaza del Obradoiro, 1
Tel. (9)81-58 22 00 – Fax (9)81-56 30 94 – Sr Martin Manzanas

Rooms 135 with telephone, bath, WC, TV and minibar; elevator. **Price** Single 18,400-19,200Pts, double 23,000-24,000Pts, suite 50,000Pts. **Meals** Breakfast 1,300Pts, served 7:00-11:00; half board 13,700Pts (per pers., 2 days min.). **Restaurant** Service 13:00-15:30, 21:00-23:30; menu 3,700Pts, also à la carte. Specialties: Merluza con almejas - Caldo gallego - Vieiras a la gallega - Solomillo de ternera gallega al horno - Tarta de santiago - Filloas rellenas de crema. **Credit cards** All major. **Pets** Dogs allowed in rooms. **Facilities** Garage (1,900Pts). **Nearby** in Santiago: Cathedral, Plaza del Obradoiro, Plaza de la Quintana, Barrio antiguo - Church Santa Maria la Real del Sarl - Pazo de Oca (manor and gardens) - Monastery of Santa Maria de Conjo. **Open** All year.

It was in 1499 that the Catholic Isabel and Fernando monarchs, established this royal hospital to shelter pilgrims. Situated on the very attractive Plaza del Obratoiro, it remains today a testimony to an epoch when history, religion, art and culture were intimately linked. Today tourists have replaced the 'walkers' on the road to Saint-Jacques, and this parador is one of the best hotels in Spain. The setting is grandiose: to list only the entry and facade in the 'plateresque' style, the four cloistered patios of the 16th- and 17th-centuries, and the former stables now used as the dining room. The rooms are exquisite, in particular Numbers 201, 202 and 204, while the 'Cardinal Suite' and the 'Royal Suite' overlook the square. The service is that of a grand hotel, attentive and discreet.

How to get there *(Map 1): facing the cathedral.*

Parador Condes de Villalba ★★★

27800 Valeriano Valdesus - Villalba (Lugo)
Tel. (9)82-51 00 11 - Fax (9)82-51 00 90
Sr Vazquez Camara

Rooms 6 with telephone, bath, WC, TV and minibar; elevator. **Price** Double
12,500-15,000Pts. **Meals** Breakfast 1,200Pts, served 8:00-11:00, full board
+ 6 375Pts (per pers., 2 days min.). **Restaurant** Service 13:00-16:00, 21:00-
23:00, menu 3,200Pts, also à la carte. Specialties: Pulpo - Filloas -
Empanadas - Lacón con grelos. **Credit cards** All major. **Pets** Dogs not allowed.
Facilities Parking. **Nearby** Lugo (cathedral and fortifications) - Chapel of
Baamonde - Monastery of Meira. **Open** All year.

It was really a very long time ago that the Los Andrade tower
defended Villalba against its attacking enemies. The
recognition due to it was almost forgotten, but the Paradores
company saved it 'in extremis' from destruction, while also
giving the region a good hotel establishment. The rooms are
very large with all the amenities required, while good regional
cuisine is served in the dining room on the ground floor. A
comfortable staging post on the road to Saint-Jacques de
Compostella.

How to get there *(Map 2): 36km north of Lugo via N6 to Rábade, then
C641.*

Parador de Monterrey ★★★

32600 Verín (Orense)
Tel. (9)88-41 00 75 - Fax (9)88-41 20 17
Sr Cardo

Rooms 23 with telephone, bath, WC, TV and minibar. **Price** Double 8,000-10,500Pts. **Meals** Breakfast 1,100Pts, served 8:00-10.30, full board + 5,950Pts (per pers., 2 days min.). **Restaurant** Service 13:30-16:00, 21:00-23:00; menu 3,000Pts, also à la carte. Specialties: Regional cooking. **Credit cards** All major. **Pets** Dogs not allowed. **Facilities** Swimming pool, garage. **Nearby** in Verín: Monterrey Castle - Church Santa Maria of Mijos - Church and Castle of Mezquita. **Open** 1. Feb - 30. Nov.

Some four kilometers from the town, this parador profits from the isolation granted to a clientele seeking maximum peace and quiet. Of recent construction but respecting the style of the region, the building dominates the valley of the Tamega, covered with vineyards, and the chateau of Monterrey. The rooms all offer equal amenities in a traditional decor, but the prettiest are those looking onto the chateau, so be sure to ask for numbers 102, 104 and 106.

How to get there (Map 2): 78km southeast of Orense via N525.

Parador Conde de Gondomar ★★★★

36300 Bayona (Pontevedra)
Tel. (9)86-35 50 00 - Fax (9)86-35 50 76
Sr Vazquez

Rooms 124 with telephone, bath, WC, TV and minibar. **Price** Double 12,000-15,500Pts. **Meals** Breakfast 1,200Pts, served 8:00-11.00, full board +6,375Pts (per pers,). **Restaurant** Service 13:30-16:00, 20:30-23:00, menu 3,200Pts, also à la carte. Specialties: Fish - Sea food - Empanadas. **Credit cards** All major. **Pets** Dogs not allowed. **Facilities** Swimming pool, tennis, garage, parking. **Nearby** Fortress (Monte Real) - Monte Groba - Road from Bayona to La Guardia. **Open** All year.

The hotel rises like an incomparable watchtower on the Monte Real peninsula, surrounded by a wall predating the Roman colonization. It was here that the galley La Pinta touched shore with the first Indians from America aboard. Its sheer size is impressive as well as the space and installations (five lounges, three dining rooms). The rooms all offer every amenity wished for. Its 18 hectares of land and 3 kilometers of walls protect it from any tourist bustle, while its sporting facilities allow one to avoid even leaving the hotel, which can be very convenient with a family holiday.

How to get there *(Map 1): 20km southwest of Vigo via C550.*

Gran Hotel de la Toja ★★★★★

36991 Isla de la Toja (Pontevedra)
Tel. (9)86-73 00 25 - Fax (9)86-73 12 01
Sr Alvarez Cordero

Rooms 200 with telephone, bath, WC, cable TV, (100 with minibar); elevator.
Price Single 16,600-23,100Pts, double 22,000-29,700Pts, suite 27,700-38,200Pts. **Meals** Breakfast included, served 7:00-11:00, full board + 9,200Pts (per pers.). **Restaurant** Service 13:30-15:00, 21:30-23:00; menu 5,000Pts, also à la carte. Specialties: Fish, sea food. **Credit cards** All major.
Pets Dogs allowed. **Facilities** Heated swimming pool, tennis, health center, golf course (9-Hole), parking. **Nearby** El Grove (Sell fish festival during the second week of Oct) - Salvora. **Open** All year.

There are the 'beach hotels' and the 'palaces on the coast', and the Gran Hotel de la Toja is certainly a 'palace on the coast'. Enjoying a privileged site on a small island of the Ria de Arosa, it has all the 'pluses' of a grand hotel: private beach, pine woods, swimming pool, tennis courts and golf besides the sea, etc.. The public rooms are luxurious: vast ceremonial lounges, but also a more intimate bar, a welcoming dining room and very comfortable rooms, even though they have more charm in the older part of the building. There is also a casino and a spa close to the hotel, which should please more than one visitor!

How to get there *(Map 1): 73km southwest of Santiago via N550 to Puente Cesures, then signs for La Toja; the hotel is located on the island.*

Parador Casa del Barón ★★★

36002 Pontevedra
Plaza Maceda - Barón, 19
Tel. (9)86-85 58 00 - Fax (9)86-85 21 95
Sr Basso Puga

Rooms 47 with telephone, bath, WC, TV, and minibar; elevator. **Price** Double 9,500-11,500Pts. **Meals** Breakfast 1,200Pts, served 8:00-11:00, full board + 6,375Pts (per pers., 2 days min.). **Restaurant** Service 13:00-16:00, 20:30-23:30; menu 3,200Pts, also à la carte. Specialties: Fish, sea food. **Credit cards** All major. **Pets** Dogs not allowed. **Facilities** Parking. **Nearby** Monastery of Lérez - Castle of Sotomayor - Mirador of Coto Redondo. **Open** All year.

The Parador Casa del Barón occupies the 'pazo' of Maceda. A 'pazo' was an ancient Galician manor house, which abandoned the military character of the Middle Age chateaux, to be inspired more by monastic or rural architecture. When in 1955 this one became a hotel, it was insisted that the original style of this aged 'pazo' should be conserved and restored. The curious kitchen (now a lounge) and the elegant staircase of the entry testify to this. The other rooms of the house are also very agreeable. The dining room opens onto the terrace and an abundantly flowered garden, while all the bedrooms are very refined. The Casa del Barón is situated in the ancient 'Barrio' (quarter) of Pontevedra, a very attractive area in this town whose surroundings are rather disappointing.

How to get there *(Map 1): 57km south of Santiago via N550; in the old part of the town.*

Parador San Telmo ★★★

36700 Túy (Pontevedra)
Avenida de Portugal
Tel. (9)86-60 03 09 - Fax (9)86-60 21 63
Sr Baños Rodriguez

Rooms 22 with telephone, bath, WC, TV, and minibar. **Price** Double 8,500-11,500Pts, suite 11,500-15,400Pts. **Meals** Breakfast 1,100Pts, served 8:00-11:00, half board + 4,100Pts, full board + 6,375Pts (per pers., 2 days min.). **Restaurant** Service 13:00-16:00, 21:00-23:30; menu 3,200Pts, also à la carte. Specialties: Pulpea Feire - Lacon con grelos. **Credit cards** All major. **Pets** Dogs not allowed. **Facilities** Swimming pool, tennis, parking. **Nearby** in Tuy: Cathedral - Romanesque church of Pexegueiro - Mirador de Aloya - Salvaterra de Miño. **Open** All year.

Built on the model of Galician houses, the hotel rises on a small promontory on the right bank of the Miño in a quiet and green countryside evoking an Irish landscape. The atmosphere reflects the environment: serene and peaceful. The bedrooms are very attractive but number 22 also has the 'extra' of a small gallery furnished in cane rattan, while the suite has a large balcony. One should note that this is also a good hotel for sampling regional specialties.

How to get there (Map 1): 34km south of Vigo via N550, towards Portugal.

Hotel Pazo El Revel ★★★

36990 Villalonga (Pontevedra)
Camino de la Iglesia
Tel. (9)86-74 30 00 – Fax (9)86-74 30 90
Sr Ansorena Garret

Rooms 22 with telephone, bath, WC, and TV. **Price** Single 6,850-7,250Pts, double 9,000-10,000Pts. **Meals** Breakfast 600Pts, served 9:00-11:00. **No restaurant. Credit cards** Visa, Eurocard, MasterCard. **Pets** Dogs not allowed. **Facilities** Swimming pool, tennis, parking. **Nearby** Monastery of Lérez - Castillo de Sotomayor - Mirador de Coto Redondo - Pontevedra - El Grove - Beaches. **Open** 1. June - 15. Sept.

This elegant 17th-century Galician residence has 22 simply appointed rooms: tiling, white walls and furniture limited to the strictly necessary, but nonetheless offering all the comfort required. The character of the house is shown more by the pretty garden with its swimming pool and tennis court, while on the covered terrace wicker armchairs await you. This place is quiet and one can listen to the birds singing, while the beaches nearby and the Romanesque churches of the region well deserve a visit.

How to get there *(Map 1): 23km north of Pontevedra via A9, exit Caldas or Pontevedra; 9km from Cambados.*

Parador de Chinchón ★★★★

28370 Chinchón (Madrid)
Avenida Generalísimo, 1
Tel. (9)1-894 08 36 – Fax (9)1-894 09 08
Sr Bertolin

Rooms 38 with air-conditioning, telephone, bath, WC, TV and minibar. **Price** Double 15,000-16,000Pts. **Meals** Breakfast 1,200Pts, served 8:00-10:00; full board + 6,950Pts (per pers.). **Restaurant** Service 13:00-15:30, 21:00-23:00; menu 3,500Pts, also à la carte. Specialties: Castilian cooking. **Credit cards** All major. **Pets** Dogs not allowed. **Facilities** Swimming pool, garage (800Pts). **Nearby** Colmenar de Oreja - Nuevo Baztàn - Alcalà de Henares - Aranjuez - Madrid. **Open** All year.

Chinchón has a main square ('Plaza Mayor') which alone deserves a visit, and the parador is not far from it. A serene atmosphere pervades this ancient convent founded by the Augustinians in the 15th century. The main staircase ceiling has retained its original frescoes and the chapel of Santa Maria del Rosario is well conserved. The simplicity of the decoration, where white and the 'azulejos' reign, gives much elegance to the lounges, dining room and bedrooms. Choose for preference suite number 8 with its terrace. The decor also lends charm to the green and flowered patios. Hidden at the bottom of the garden, where the kitchen garden used to be, there is an attractive swimming pool and bar, both inviting relaxation, as with the little corners under the trees and bamboos, among the flowers and fountains.

How to get there *(Map 13): 52km southeast of Madrid via N3 to Puente de Azganda, then C300; close to the Plaza Mayor.*

Hotel Santa Maria del Paular ★★★★

28741 Rascafria (Madrid)
Carret. de Cotos, km 26, 5
Tel. (9)1-869 10 11/12 – Fax (9)1-869 10 06 – Sr González Otero

Rooms 58 with air-conditioning, telephone, bath or shower, WC and cable TV.
Price Single 10,000-13,000Pts, double 14,500-19,000Pts. **Meals** Breakfast
1,600Pts, served 8:00-11:00, full board + 9,000Pts (per pers., 3 days min.).
Restaurant Service 13:30-16:00, 21:00-23:30, menu 4,500Pts, also à la carte.
Specialties: Judiones de la Granja con Matanza – Cordero Lechal – Asado al
Horno de leña – Cochinillo frito – Buñuelos al bon – Pastelerìa. **Credit cards** All
major. **Pets** Dogs not allowed. **Facilities** Heated swimming pool, tennis, bike,
billiards, parking. **Nearby** Monastery del Paular – Skiing in Puerto de
Navacerrada. **Open** 1. Feb - 11. Dec.

At the foot of the Sierra de Guadarrama beside the River
Lozoya, and scarcely 85 kilometers from Madrid, we find
ourselves at the very picturesque site of Santa Maria del Paular.
Even though classified as a historical monument, this ancient
monastery of the Carthusians dating from 1390 was abandoned.
It was only in 1948 that part of it became a parador, and in
1952 that some Benedictine monks installed themselves in the
monastery, to give life back to this beautiful ensemble. In
passing through the main archway, similar to a triumphal arch,
one comes to the Ave Maria patio surrounded by a colonnade
supporting the red-brick building. Inside the same sobriety and
the same good taste are found, while behind a garden leads to
the swimming pool and tennis court.

How to get there *(Map 1): 85km north of Madrid via N1; at km 69 take C604.*

Ritz Hotel ★★★★★

28014 Madrid
Plaza de la Lealtad, 5
Tel. (9)1-521 28 57 - Fax (9)1-532 87 76 - Sr Jordàn

Rooms 156 with air-conditioning, telephone, bath, WC, cable TV, safe and minibar; elevator. **Price** Single 37,000Pts, double 49,500-60,500Pts, suite 80,000-176,000Pts. **Meals** Breakfast 2,700Pts, served 8:00-11:00. **Restaurant** Service 13:30-16:00, 20:30-24:00; carte 4,000-5,200Pts. Specialties: Cocido madrileño - Paella Ritz. **Credit cards** All major. **Pets** Dogs allowed in the rooms. **Nearby** Palacio del Prado - Castillo de los duques de l'Infantado in Manzanares el Real - El Paular Monastery - Villages of the Sierra Pobre (Talamanca de Jarama, Torrelaguna, Patones, the Sierra Pobre de Torrelagana towards El Berrueco) - Valle de los Caídos - Monastery of the Escorial - Valle de los Caìdos; Puerta de Hierro golf course (18-Hole). **Open** All year.

Bearing the name that has become the symbol of 'grand luxe' hotels, the Ritz of Madrid was built on the initiative of Alfonso XIII. Totally renovated but more faithful than ever to its initial decoration, the result is striking: the sumptuous carpets from the Real Fábrica that cover all the floors are superb, and so precious that a full-time repairer is employed. The gardens and terrace have been reopened, while the menu and the cellars of the famous restaurant have been yet further improved. In the rooms one always finds those Ritz details: sumptuous bouquets of flowers, the initialed towels of the hotel (that make one doubt one's honesty !), and the baskets of exquisite fruits. Even if not staying at the Ritz you can always take tea in the Royal ('Real') Lounge, lunch in the garden, cocktail on the terrace, or dinner in the most beautiful restaurant in Madrid.

How to get there *(Map 13): facing the Prado Museum.*

Palace Hotel ★★★★★

28014 Madrid
Plaza de las Cortes, 7
Tel. (9)1-429 75 51 - Fax (9)1-429 82 66 - Sr Bergés

Rooms 480 and 20 suites with air-conditioning, telephone, bath, WC, cable TV, safe and minibar; elevator; handicap access. **Price** Single 21,000Pts, double 40,000Pts, suite 75,000-175,000Pts. **Meals** Breakfast 2,750Pts, served 7:15-11:00, full board + 6,750Pts (per pers.). **Restaurant** Service 13:00-16:00, 20:15-23:30; closed Sat and Aug; menus 6,750-13,500Pts, also à la carte. **Credit cards** All major. **Pets** Dogs allowed in the rooms. **Facilities** Hairdresser. **Nearby** Palacio del Prado - Castillo de los duques de l'Infantado in Manzanares el Real - El Paular Monastery - Villages of the Sierra Pobre (Talamanca de Jarama, Torrelaguna, Patones, the Sierra Pobre de Torrelagana towards El Berrueco) - Valle de los Caídos - Monastery of the Escorial - Valle de los Caìdos; Puerta de Hierro golf course (18-Hole). **Open** All year.

Admirably well situated, the Palace deploys its immense facade in the face of the square Canovas del Castillo, between the Prado Museum and the Congress. King Alfonso XIII opened it in 1912. Prestigious, it has been selected by many personalities of the century from Mata Hari to Richard Nixon, among many others. Its majestic hallway leads to one of the most beautiful lounges, 'La Rotonda', where a series of double neo–classical columns supports a magnificent cupola decorated with Art Nouveau tiles. A lamp with its palms of crystal hangs down from the ceiling to complete this superb 1900's decor. The bedrooms are perfect, while a luxury of good taste makes every space into an exceptional location. This hotel is for those refined friends who do not flinch at the prices!

How to get there (Map 13): facing the Prado Museum.

Villa Real ★★★★

28014 Madrid
Plaza de las Cortes, 10
Teél. (9)1-420 37 67 - Fax (9)1-420 25 47 - Sr Garcia

Rooms 115 with air-conditioning, telephone, bath, WC, cable TV, safe and minibar; elevator. **Price** Single 17,000 Pts (week-end)-26,500Pts, double 17,000 (week-end)-34,400Pts, suite 25,000Pts-65,000Pts. **Meals** Breakfast included (buffet), served 8:00-11:00. **Restaurant** Service 13:30-15:30, 20:30-23:30; menu 5,000Pts, also à la carte. **Credit cards** All major. **Pets** Dogs not allowed. **Facilities** Sauna (1,200Pts), garage (1,600Pts). **Nearby** Palacio del Prado - Castillo de los duques de l'Infantado in Manzanares el Real - El Paular Monastery - Villages of the Sierra Pobre (Talamanca de Jarama, Torrelaguna, Patones, the Sierra Pobre de Torrelagana towards El Berrueco) - Valle de los Caídos - Monastery of the Escorial - Valle de los Caìdos; Puerta de Hierro golf course (18-Hole). **Open** All year.

In default of any charming small hotel in Madrid, we have selected this recent four-star house. With its 1900s' decor, it is very well situated facing the Prado Museum at the very heart of the cultural and financial quarter of the capital. Inside there is the atmosphere of a grand hotel: vast lounges luxuriously decorated and a cosy bar. The huge and classical rooms are very attractive, with very well equiped bathrooms, and which still have that freshness so lacking in certain bedrooms of the 'palaces'. The service is attentive, the welcome friendly and not at all starchy.

How to get there *(Map 13): in the city center, facing the Prado Museum.*

Hotel Wellington ★★★★★

28001 Madrid
Velásquez, 8
Tel. (9)1-575 44 00 - Fax (9)1-576 41 64 - Sr Lobo

Rooms 195 and 19 suites with air-conditioning, telephone, bath, WC, cable TV, safe and minibar; elevator. **Price** Single 16,000Pts (week-end)-20,750Pts, double 17,500Pts (week-end)-33,250Pts, suite 49,500-33,250Pts. **Meals** Breakfast 2,200Pts, served 7:00-11:00. **Restaurant** "El Fogon" Service 13:30-16:00, 21:30-22:30; carte 5,300-6,000Pts. Specialties: International cooking. **Credit cards** All major. **Pets** Dogs not allowed. **Facilities** Swimming pool, garage (2,013Pts). **Nearby** Palacio del Prado - Castillo de los duques de l'Infantado in Manzanares el Real - El Paular Monastery - Villages of the Sierra Pobre (Talamanca de Jarama, Torrelaguna, Patones, the Sierra Pobre de Torrelagana towards El Berrueco) - Valle de los Caídos - Monastery of the Escorial - Valle de los Caìdos; Puerta de Hierro golf course (18-Hole). **Open** All year.

The Wellington is a luxurious hotel where a calm and cosy atmosphere reigns. The rooms are spacious and well equiped, and have beautiful bathrooms in marble. Those with windows over the Via Velásquez are protected with double glazing to assure perfect quiet. Choose first those rooms overlooking the interior garden and swimming pool, or even better those on the top floor with their own small terraces. One will linger happily at the hotel bar with its English style: panelling, copper work and lamps make it a particularly warm corner. The rustic decor of the dining room is perhaps rather surprising in such surroundings: beams, white walls and hunting trophees, but it is nonetheless attractive.

How to get there *(Map 13): near the Parque del Retiro.*

Hotel Monaco ★

80004 Madrid
Calle Barbieri, 5
Tel. (9)1-522 46 30 – Fax (9)1-521 16 01
Sr Martin Nunes

Rooms 32 with telephone, bath or shower, WC, TV; elevator. **Price** Single 6,000Pts, double 9,000Pts, triple 10,500Pts. **Meals** Breakfast 350-450Pts, served 8:00-10:00. **Restaurant** See pp. 204-206. **Credit cards** Amex, Visa, Eurocard, MasterCard. **Pets** Dogs allowed. **Nearby** Palacio del Prado - Castillo de los duques de l'Infantado in Manzanares el Real - El Paular Monastery - Villages of the Sierra Pobre (Talamanca de Jarama, Torrelaguna, Patones, the Sierra Pobre de Torrelagana towards El Berrueco) - Valle de los Caídos - Monastery of the Escorial - Valle de los Caìdos; Puerta de Hierro golf course (18-Hole). **Open** All year.

In a small street behind the Grand Via, the Monaco is a hotel whose charm comes a lot from the 'démodé' and kitsch side of its decoration. In the entry hallway the marble floors mix the pink neon lights indicating the bar, and also lighting a curious fresco. All this is intriguing enough and prods one to discover the rest of the hotel. The bedrooms may either attract or disconcert depending on tastes, and one finds many mirrors painted with columns or decorated with false plaster curtains. One has to insist that the Monaco will very soon need a major general renovation (the bedroom paintwork is flaking and bathrooms are dated), otherwise the frontier between charm and old age will definitely be crossed.

How to get there *(Map 13): near the Gran Via.*

Hotel Inglés ★★★★

28014 Madrid
Echegaray, 8
Tel. (9)1-429 65 51 – Fax (9)1-420 24 23
Sr Antonio Marco

Rooms 58 with telephone, bath or shower, WC, cable TV; elevator. **Price** Single 7,480Pts, double 10,700Pts, triple 13,600Pts. **Meals** Breakfast 500Pts, served 7:30-11:00. **Restaurant** See pp. 204-206. **Credit cards** All major. **Pets** Dogs not allowed. **Facilities** Garage (1,200Pts). **Nearby** Palacio del Prado - Castillo de los duques de l'Infantado in Manzanares el Real - El Paular Monastery - Villages of the Sierra Pobre (Talamanca de Jarama, Torrelaguna, Patones, the Sierra Pobre de Torrelagana towards El Berrueco) - Valle de los Caídos - Monastery of the Escorial - Valle de los Caìdos; Puerta de Hierro golf course (18-Hole). **Open** All year.

In the heart of the city and only two paces from old Madrid, the Calle Echegaray is a very lively street full of small restaurants. It is here that the Hotel Inglés is to be found. All the bedrooms have been recently renovated and offer full amenities, although one rather regrets their somewhat clinic-like floors. The 'British' aspect evoked by the name of the hotel is found in the discreetly lit lounge where deep leather armchairs await you. Another advantage of the hotel is the parking, and when you know Madrid and its traffic, this is a huge 'plus'. Finally, with more than 100 years of age, the Hotel Inglés is professional and efficient, while the prices are reasonable for Madrid, where charm is to be found in the palaces above all.

How to get there *(Map 13): near the Puerta del Sol.*

Hotel Ayestaran ★

31870 Lecumberri (Navarra)
Calle Aralarso
Tel. (9)48-50 41 27 - Fax (9)48-50 41 27 - Sr Ayestaran Oquinena

Rooms 90 (54 with bath); 15 with bath and WC. **Price** Double 3,300-5,500-6,500Pts. **Meals** Breakfast 400Pts, served 8:30-11:00; half board + 3,600-4,785Pts, full board + 5,060-5,450Pts (per pers.). **Restaurant** Service 13:30-15:30, 21:00-22:30; menu 1,550Pts, also à la carte. Specialties: Alcachofas al jamòn - Meat. **Credit cards** Visa, Eurocard, MasterCard. **Pets** Dogs allowed in rooms. **Facilities** Swimming pool, tennis. **Nearby** Fishing - Walking. **Open** 20. Jan - 20. Dec.

Getting away from the coast and entering the real Basque country, the Hotel Ayestaran is lodged in two buildings, one residence for summer and a second for winter, on either side of the road. This latter is rather too busy at the moment, but within two years it will be diverted. In the meantime the hotel does not lack for charm, all white with red shutters in summertime, but all white with green shutters in winter. Its first hundred years have just been celebrated. The hotel corridors are filled with Basque furniture from the start of the century, while the bedrooms are simple and furnished with old beds from the region. Bathrooms have been renovated. Those rooms on the road are all double-glazed. The 100-year-old trees of the garden shade a swimming pool and tennis court. The winter hotel is more traditional with its typical dining room and open fireplace, its woodwork and furniture. Once again the bathrooms have been renovated. The welcome is among the most friendly.

How to get there (Map 6): 56km south of San Sebastián via N1 to Tolosa, then N240.

Hospederia de Leyre ★★

31410 Monasterio de Leyre (Navarra)
Tel. (9)48-88 41 00 - Fax (9)48-88 41 37
Sr Perez

Rooms 32 with telephone, bath or shower and WC. **Price** Single 4,000-4,400Pts, double 7,000-8,500Pts. **Meals** Breakfast 700Pts, served 8:30-10:30, half board + 2,750Pts, + 3,840Pts (per pers., 2 days min.). **Restaurant** With air-conditioning. Service 12:30-14:00, 19:30-21:00, menu 2,050Pts, also à la carte. Specialties: Regional cooking. **Credit cards** All major. **Pets** Dogs not allowed. **Facilities** Parking. **Nearby** Monastery of Leyre - Pamplona. **Open** All year.

In the Sierra de Leyre at the end of a winding and steep road, this ancient monastery rises up in the midst of a site of great beauty. The panorama over the artificial lake of Yesa and its environment of small hills is splendid. Considered in the 11th century as the great spiritual center of Navarre, and then abandoned in the 19th century, the monastery is now one of the most important historical monuments of the region. The hotel has been installed in the 17th- and 18th-century parts of the building, which have been renovated, and it offers 30 rooms, all simply furnished but comfortable. In the lounges you will appreciate the quiet that characterizes this establishment full of charm.

How to get there *(Map 6): 51km southeast of Pamplona via N240 to Yesa, then take small road to the left.*

Hotel Europa ★★★

31001 Pamplona (Navarra)
Espoz y Mina, 11
Tel. (9)48-22 18 00 - Fax (9)48-22 92 35
Familla Idoate

Rooms 25 with air-conditioning, telephone, bath, WC, TV, and minibar; elevator. **Price** Double 7,500-12,900Pts. **Meals** Breakfast 850Pts, served 8:00-10.30, full board + 5,250Pts (per pers.). **Restaurant** Service 12:30-15:00, 2o:30-23:00; closed Sun; carte 4,300-6,200Pts. Specialties: Lenguado relleno de cigalitas con crema de espàrragos - Cordero relleno de lechezuelas. **Credit cards** All major. **Pets** Dogs not allowed. **Nearby** in Pamplona: Cathedral, Museum of Navarra - Feria (July) - Santiago de Compostella road in Navarra (Roncesvalles, Pamplona, Obanos, Puenta la Reina, Estella, Los Arcos, Torres del Rìo) - Ulzama golf course (9-Hole). **Open** All year.

Pamplona is famous for its festivals and notably its 'Encierro', when bulls are let loose in the streets of the town before the bullfights in the arenas on the same afternoon. Gourmet 'aficionados' know the Europa above all for its gastronomic restaurant preparing an excellent cuisine from the market - and for its wine cellar. This fully renovated hotel also makes you appreciate the 'know-how' of the family team. A classical but also modern decor which favors above all comfort and service : everything is impeccable, well thought-out, discreet, stylish - and also a little bit formal, as so often with the ambiance of any well-known restaurant. But one would be wrong to complain about too much perfection !

How to get there *(Map 6): 80km south from San Sebastian.*

Mesòn del Peregrino ★★

31100 Puente La Reina (Navarra)
Carretera de Pamplona, 11
Tel. (9)48-34 00 75 - Fax (9)48-34 11 90
Angel Combero - Nina Sedana

Rooms 15 with air-conditioning, telephone, bath, WC and TV. **Price** Double 8,000Pts, suite 25,000Pts. **Meals** Breakfast 1,300Pts, served 8:00-10:30. **Restaurant** Service 13:00-15:00, 20:30-23:00; menu 3,500Pts, also à la carte. **Credit cards** All major. **Pets** Dogs allowed. **Facilities** Swimming pool, parking. **Nearby** Pamplona - Feria of Pamplona (July) - Santiago de Compostella road in Navarra (Roncesvalles, Pamplona, Obanos, Puenta la Reina, Estella, Los Arcos, Torres del Rìo) - Ulzama golf course (9-Hole). **Open** All year except Christmas.

If you are rather fearful of the too lively nights of the Saint Firmin festival in Pamplona, then take refuge some twenty kilometers away at Puente La Reina, a strategic staging post on the road to Santiago de Compostela. At the Meson del Peregrino everything is done to attract you, and all is thought out to satisfy your well-being: reception, comfort, decor and gastronomy should create that harmony to satisfy all your senses. It is true that the old stone house is pretty, the large dining room opening onto the garden is welcoming and warm, the cuisine appetizing, the garden with its swimming pool restful. Nina and Angelo practise the art of receiving well admirably, and this is a very attractive address to seek out.

How to get there (Map 6): 24km southwestfrom Pamplona.

Parador Principe de Viana ★★★

31390 Olite (Navarra)
Plaza de los Teobaldos, 2
Tel. (9)48-74 00 00 - Fax (9)48-74 02 01
Sr Montero Moreiro

Rooms 43 with air-conditioning, telephone, bath, WC, TV and minibar; elevator. **Price** Double 11,000-13,000Pts. **Meals** Breakfast 1,200Pts served 8:00-10:30, full board + 6,375Pts (per pers., 3 days min.). **Restaurant** Service 13:00-16:00, 20:30-23:00; menu 3,200Pts, also à la carte. Specialties: Regional cooking. **Credit cards** All major. **Pets** Dogs not allowed. **Nearby** in Olite: Castle, Church of Santa Maria la Real, Church of San Pedro - Monastery of Oliva - Pamplona. **Open** All year.

Installed in the residential part of the very beautiful chateau of the Kings of Navarre, the parador opens onto a small, quiet and sunny square planted with trees. The decor preserves the medieval character of the building and gives it all its charm. In addition, thanks to the stained glass windows, a soft and warm light gives the house an atmosphere of calm and meditation. The rooms have been installed in a recently rebuilt part of the building: they are sober and comfortable, but lack however the charm of the lounges.

How to get there *(Map 6): 43km south of Pamplona via N140, or via A15.*

Parador de Argómaniz ***

01192 Argómaniz-Vitoria (Alava)
Carretera N 1
Tél. (9)45 28 22 00 - Fax (9)45 28 28 22
Sr Hernandez Garcia

Rooms 54 with telephone, bath, WC, TV and minibar; elevator. **Price** Double 10,000-11,500Pts. **Meals** Breakfast 1,200Pts, served 8:00-11:00; half board + 6,375Pts (per pers.). **Restaurant** Service 13:00-16:00, 20:30-23:00; menu 3,200Pts, also à la carte. Specialties: regional cooking **Credit cards** All major. **Pets** Dogs not allowed. **Facilities** Parking. **Nearby** in Vitoria: Church of Santa Maria and the museum - Salinas de Añana - Sanctuary of Estibaliz. **Open** All year.

Before giving battle to the Spanish and British at Vitoria, the Emperor Napoleon lodged in this 17th-century building. The earlier promenade with arcades has been transformed into the reception hall and one can still admire the original columns. The many lounges contribute to the hotel's comfortable ambiance, allowing you to enjoy the quiet of the building. On the top floor, under the eaves, the woodwork has been left uncovered, and here the dining room is to be found. The rooms are placed in the two modern wings, and are soberly decorated. Comfortable and very light, they also have small corner lounges. From the windows one can see the hill of Estibaliz with its monastery, and in the distance Vitoria, the capital of the province.

How to get there (Map 5): 15km east of Vitoria via N1.

Hotel Arocena ★★★

20740 Cestona (Guipúzcoa)
Paseo de San Juan, 12
Tel. (9)43-14 70 40 – Fax (9)43-14 79 78
Sr Arocena

Rooms 110 with telephone, bath, WC and TV. **Price** Single 4,300-5,900Pts, double 7,200-9,900Pts, 4 pers. 12,500-15,500Pts. **Meals** Breakfast 750Pts, served 8:00-11:00, full board + 3,700Pts (per pers.). **Restaurant** Service 13:00-15:00, 21:00-23:00; menu 2,400Pts, also à la carte. Specialties: Fish. **Credit cards** All major. **Pets** Dogs allowed in the rooms. **Facilities** Swimming pool, tennis, sauna, fitness club, garage, parking. **Nearby** Therms - Sanctuary of San Ignacio de Loyala; San Sebastián - San Sebastián and Jaizkibel golf courses (18-Hole). **Open** 15. Jan - 15. Dec.

This old hotel from the last century is in a plain lined with gently sloping hills that have always attracted those taking the waters. In this hotel they also found the charm they had come in search of, and the benefits of the medicinal waters of Cestona. Huge gardens surround the swimming pool, tennis court and park. The hotel's entry is well done with its interior gallery all in wood. Sadly, many of the rooms have been over-renovated in order to offer more amenities, but some have been preserved from this. The dining room has also been preserved and is set on two levels, with the second particularly attractive with stone columns, grand piano and flowered curtains.

How to get there (Map 5): 34km southwest of San Sebastián.

Hotel Obispo ★★★

20280 Fuenterrabia - Hondarribia (Guipúzcoa)
Plaza del Obispo
Tel. (9)43-64 54 00 - Fax (9)43-64 23 86
Sr Alza

Rooms 25 with telephone, bath, WC, TV, and minibar. **Price** Double 10,000-14,000Pts, suite 12,000-16,000Pts. **Meals** Breakfast 900Pts, served 8:00-11:00. **Restaurant** Service 20:00-23:00; closed Sun night and 15. Dec - 15. Jan; carte. Specialties: Fish. **Credit cards** Amex, Visa, Eurocard, MasterCard. **Pets** Dogs not allowed. **Nearby** Ermita de San Marcial (view) - Road from Fuenterrabia to San Juan via Jaizkibel (view) - San Sebastián; San Sebastián and Jaizkibel golf courses (18-Hole). **Open** All year.

This new hotel is in one of the beautiful Renaissance houses that resisted the siege by the Prince de Condé in 1638. Indeed, Fuentarrabia does not lack for history and qualities, while this charming town, only some twenty kilometers from San Sebastián, no doubt profits from the proximity of the Basque coast to attract a clientele who prefer getting away from the tourist crowd in the summer months. Inside the hotel the austerity of the stone and wood, traditionally used in the regional architecture, has been well exploited. The decoration creates a warm and even snug atmosphere: everywhere the pale wood furniture, the flowery fabrics, parquet floors and large cord carpets form a rustic ambiance in good taste. The amenities have not been forgotten, while the welcome and service are professional.

How to get there (Map 6): 18km southwest of St-Jean-de-Luz.

Hotel Pampinot ★★★

20280 Fuenterrabia - Hondarribia (Guipúzcoa)
Calle Mayor, 3
Tel. (9)43-64 06 00 - Fax (9)43-64 51 28
Sra Alvarez

Rooms 8 with telephone, bath, WC and TV. **Price** Double 10,500-14,000Pts, suite 15,000-17,000Pts. **Meals** Breakfast 1,200Pts, served 8:00-11:00. **Restaurant** See p. 206. **Credit cards** All major. **Pets** Dogs allowed. **Nearby** Ermita de San Marcial (view) - Road from Fuenterrabia to San Juan via Jaizkibel (view) - San Sebastián; San Sebastián and Jaizkibel golf courses (18-Hole). **Open** 1. Dec - 30. Oct.

This is a former private house from the 18th century, in the heart of the very pretty town of Hondarribia. The entry hall with its walls of bare stone displays carefully chosen antiques, while a beautiful columned staircase leads to the rooms upstairs. Decorated more simply but all personalized with taste, the rooms are attractive and offer all the amenities. A quiet hotel offering a friendly welcome, where the absence of a restaurant adds to the peaceful impression. Our only regret: the 'airport-lounge-style' background music !

How to get there (Map 6): 18km southwest of St-Jean-de-Luz.

Hotel Maria Cristina ★★★★★

20004 San Sebastián-Donostia (Guipúzcoa)
Paseo de la Republíca Argentina, 4
Tel. (9)43 42 49 00 - Fax (9)43 42 39 14

Rooms 139 with air-conditioning, telephone, bath, WC, cable TV and minibar; elevator. **Price** Single 18,000-23,000Pts, double 24,500-39,000Pts, suite 55,600-88,500Pts. **Meals** Breakfast 2,000Pts served 7:00-11:00. **Restaurant** Service 13:30-15:30, 21:00-23:30; carte 5,700Pts. Specialties: Regional and international cooking. **Credit cards** All major. **Pets** Dogs not allowed. **Nearby** Monte Ulia - Monte Urgull - Monte Igueldo; San Sebastián and Jaizkibel golf courses (18-Hole). **Open** All year.

This hotel evokes all the charms of the 'Belle Epoque', but it has been entirely renovated to satisfy a wealthy and refined clientele who appreciate luxury and comfort. There is tradition in the pseudo-Louis XV and Empire decors of the lounges and bedrooms, but contemporary efficiency elsewhere, as witnessed by the quality of amenities in the bathrooms and the immense kitchens. Its situation in the heart of the city is not the least of advantages. From the rooms, each with its own small balcony, one looks over the River Urumea, and there is a fine view of the Victoria Eugénia Theater that hosts the International Cinema Festival each September.

How to get there (Map 5): in the city center.

Hotel Monte Igueldo ★★★★

20008 San Sebastián–Donostia (Guipúzcoa)
Tel. (9)43-21 02 11 – Fax (9)43-21 50 28
Sra Pascual

Rooms 125 with telephone, bath, WC, cable TV; elevator. **Price** Single 12,400-13,600Pts, double 15,500-17,000Pts, triple 21,500-23,000Pts. **Meals** Breakfast 1,050Pts served 7:30-11:00. **Restaurant** with air-conditioning, service 13:00-15:00, 20:30-23:00; menu 2,200-2,500Pts. Specialties: Fish, chipirones. **Credit cards** All major. **Pets** Dogs not allowed. **Facilities** Swimming pool, parking. **Nearby** Monte Ulia - Monte Urgull - Monte Igueldo; San Sebastián and Jaizkibel golf courses (18-Hole). **Open** All year.

Built in 1967 on the summit of a hill dominating San Sebastián, this hotel is above all appreciated for its exceptional site. One has taken advantage of its beauty by giving the lounge and dining room huge bay windows looking over both sea and city. One might wish the bedrooms decorated with more taste, but nearly all of them have balconies except those on the corners, but these are brighter and have better access to the panoramic view: San Sebastián, with in the background the first peaks of the Pyrenees and, on a fine day, Biarritz in the distance. It is all superb! On the large roof-terrace there is a beautiful swimming pool and self-service restaurant, much appreciated in summer. One does regret however that the peace of the site is sometimes disturbed by the small amusement park close by.

How to get there (Map 5): 5km west of San Sebastián, towards Monte Igueldo; a funicular railway ascends from the 'Ondarreta' beach to the amusement park.

Hotel de Londres y de Inglaterra ★★★★

20007 San Sebastián-Donostia (Guipúzcoa)
Zubieta, 2
Tel. (9)43-42 69 89 – Fax (9)43-42 00 31
Sr Vriarte

Rooms 133 with air-conditioning, telephone, bath, WC, cable TV, safe and minibar; elevator. **Price** Single 14,300-16,000Pts, double 17,800-20,000Pts, suite 22,000-27,000Pts. **Meals** Breakfast 1,100Pts served 7:00-11:00, half board + 3,450 Pts, full board + 8,050Pts (per pers.). **Restaurant** service 13:00-15:30, 20:45-23:15; menu 1,900Pts, also à la carte. Specialties: Basque cooking. **Credit cards** All major. **Pets** Dogs not allowed. **Nearby** Monte Ulia - Monte Urgull - Monte Igueldo; San Sebastián and Jaizkibel golf courses (18-Hole). **Open** All year.

This hotel enjoyed a glorious period when the royal family came to San Sebastián for the summer months. The hotel overlooks the La Concha beach (enclosed by rocks), which was then very much in fashion. If this same fashion has now rather forgotten it, the hotel has however lost nothing of its splendor. There is still something of pride in this historic edifice. The service cannot take too much care, while the bedrooms are those of the classical grand hotel. One can hire a small boat from the hotel to cross to the small island of Santa Clara, which is always amusing.

How to get there (Map 5): in the city center.

Hotel Jatetxen Urrutitxo ★

20400 Tolosa (Guipúzcoa)
Kondero Aldapa, 7
Tel. (9)43 67 38 22 - Fax (9) 43 67 34 28
Sr Blanco Gordo

Rooms 7 with telephone, shower, WC and TV. **Price** Single 5,000-5,500Pts, double 7,750-8,500Pts. **Meals** Breakfast 650Pts served 8:00-10:00, full board + 3,500Pts (per pers.). **Restaurant** service 13:00-14:30, 20:30-22:30; menu 1,750Pts, also à la carte. Specialties: Regional and international cooking. **Credit cards** All major. **Pets** Dogs not allowed. **Facilities** Parking. **Nearby** Monte Ulia - Monte Urgull - Monte Igueldo; San Sebastián and Jaizkibel golf courses (18-Hole). **Open** All year except 1. - 15. Jan.

An all-white-and-red house, and all Basque in the midst of the country: such is the Hotel Jatetxen Urrutitxo. The house was built in 1920 and restructured into a hotel in 1987. Both decoration and atmosphere have a lot of charm, with a small touch of French style. The bedrooms lack any great embellishments but are all in good taste, while the bathrooms lack no amenities. The restaurant is also good and the welcome friendly. This is a good halting place when discovering the Basque country.

How to get there *(Map 5): 27km south of San Sebastián via N1.*

Hosterìa de Señorio de Biskaia ★★

48130 Bakio (Vizcaya)
Calle Cirarda
Tel. (9)4-619 47 25 – Fax (9)4-619 47 25
Sr Aldecoa

Rooms 16 with telephone, shower, WC and TV. **Price** Single 6,470-7,460Pts, double 7,975-8,975Pts. **Meals** Breakfast included, served 8:30-10:30, half board 8,420 (1 pers.)-11,875 (2 pers.), full board 9,710Pts (1 pers.)-14,445Pts (2 pers.). **Restaurant** service 13:00-14:30, 20:30-22:00; carte. Specialties: Spanish and Basque cooking. **Credit cards** Amex, Visa, Eurocard, MasterCard. **Pets** Dogs allowed. **Facilities** Parking. **Nearby** Bilbao; Bilbaina golf courses (18-Hole). **Open** All year except 7.Jan - 1. Mar.

It is difficult not to succumb to the charm of this large house with its pink stone and white balconies, converted some years ago into a small hotel. A rare balance is found here between a respect for the authentic and comfort. Its thick walls shelter a small restaurant and convivial bar on the ground floor, where they will serve you a few pinchos, among other drinks. A wooden staircase leads to the very well-arranged rooms, bright and pretty with their white walls and clear parquet floors. The bathrooms are perfect, while the suite on the upper floor has a veranda-lounge. The ultimate of romanticism, in the hotel park there is a small and shaded island reached via an aging wooden bridge. We should add that there is a very friendly welcome as well. Proximity to the Bakio beach, a paradise for surfers, is yet another 'plus' for this little hotel of charm.

How to get there *(Map 5): 26km north of Bilbao.*

Andorra Park Hotel ★★★★

Andorra la Vieja (Principality of Andorra)
Les Canals
Tel. 376/ 8 209 79 – Fax 376/ 8 209 83
Sr Antoni Cruz

Rooms 40 with telephone, bath, WC, TV and minibar; elevator. **Price** Single 6,500-18,500Pts, double 7,400-18,500Pts. **Meals** Breakfast included, served 7:30-11:00; half board + 12,200-24,400, full board 16,350-28,600Pts (per pers.). **Restaurant** Service 13:30-15:30, 21:00-22:30; carte 5,700Pts. Specialties: Spanish and French cooking. **Credit cards** All major. **Pets** Dogs not allowed. **Facilities** Swimming pool, tennis, golf practise, parking. **Nearby** Skiing - Walking - Seu d'Urgell. **Open** All year.

The Andorra Park Hotel is a real oasis in this city suburb recently converted into a vast commercial center. The hotel is an excellent staging post and address on the way to Barcelona, or if you want to ski in the small resorts of the Principality. The result of an attractive restoration, three types of rooms are offered, and prices vary as to whether they have terraces or views over the valley. The decor is classical of a grand hotel, but modern and luxurious. The park surrounding the hotel is magnificent: carefully mown lawns, an admirable swimming pool carved out of the rock itself and with the mountains as back-drop, tennis, practice range - everything is done so that you get to know this 'natural' side of the town. There is also the restaurant opening out wide and directly onto the long terrace and garden. But the 'unconditionals of modern consumption' can also be reassured - the hotel could not resist having its own direct access to the "Pyrenees" department store !

How to get there (Map 8): 220km north of Barcelona.

PRINCIPALITY OF ANDORRA

Hostal San Pere

El Tarter/Soldeu (Principality of Andorra)
Prat dels Nogués
Tel. 376/ 8 510 87– Fax 376/ 8 510 87

Rooms 6 with telephone, bath and WC. **Price** Double 9,000-13,000Pts. **Meals**
Breakfast included, served 7:30-11:00. **Restaurant** Service 13:30-15:30,
21:00-22:30; closed Sun night and Mon; carte 5,000Pts. Specialties: Meat.
Credit cards All major. **Pets** Dogs allowed in the rooms. **Facilities** Parking.
Nearby Skiing - Walking - Seu d'Urgell. **Open** All year.

Half way between the French frontier at Pas de la Casa and
Andorra la Vieja, the Hostal de San Pere is a genuine
mountain address magnificently sited at the foot of the Tarter
ski runs, while one can enjoy here the peace and quiet and
view of the summits. The house has been well restored and
provides many small corners for sitting undisturbed by the open
fires, or even at the bar to enjoy the view over so much nature.
Very rustic and very warm, the restaurant lets you discover the
specialties of Andorra and more particularly its grilled meats.
The rooms are in the same style: with beams, timbered, some
with sloping ceilings – all are different and comfortable. This is
a charming and welcoming inn.

How to get there (Map 8): 220km north of Barcelona.

Xalet Ritz Hotel

Sispony/La Massana (Principality of Andorra)
Prat dels Nogués
Tel. 376/ 8 378 77– Fax 376/ 8 377 20

Rooms 50 with telephone, bath, WC and TV; elevator. **Price** Single 7,500-14,000Pts, double 10,000-19,000Pts. **Meals** Breakfast included, served 7:30-11:00, half board 7,500-12,500, full board 9,500-15,000Pts (per pers.). **Restaurant** Service 13:30-15:30, 21:00-22:30; menu 3,500Pts. Specialties: Regional cooking. **Credit cards** All major. **Pets** Dogs allowed in the rooms. **Facilities** Swimming pool, paddle-pool, garage, parking. **Nearby** Skiing - Walking - Seu d'Urgell. **Open** All year.

One should forget the fair-time ambiance of the streets of the 'capital' of the Principality, to discover the snow-covered summits of the Pyrenees, the woods and paths alongside the mountain torrents. Just a few minutes away from all such frenzy, the Xalet Ritz is found at the entry of the valley of the Valerà, on an ideal site to profit from the mountain environment. It is a stone building typical of the region, and offering many possibilities for relaxation more or less sporting : from the hotel itself one can follow the high mountain trails, reach the ski slopes in less than a quarter of an hour, or enjoy the swimming pool and large garden in the warmer season. The rooms offer all the comforts with the snug decor of an alpine style. This is a good alternative staging post at more reasonable prices.

How to get there (Map 8): 220km north of Barcelona.

Hotel Bahia Vista ★★★

03730 Jàvea (Alicante)
Portichol 76
Tel. (9)6-579 47 80 – Fax (9)6-647 09 95 – Sr Dickens

Rooms 17 (11 with telephone) with bath. **Price** Single and double 7,600-9,500Pts. **Meals** Breakfast 550Pts, served 8:30-11:30; half board + 1,725Pts, full board + 2,820Pts (per pers., 3 days min.). **Restaurant** Service 13:00-15:00, 20:00-23:00; menu 1,900Pts, also à la carte. Specialties: regional and international cooking. **Credit cards** All major. **Pets** Dogs not allowed. **Facilities** Swimming pool, parking. **Nearby** Cabo de San Antonio - Cabo de la Nao - Costa de Azahar to Valencia - Tosalet golf course (9-Hole). **Open** All year.

Between Jàvea and the Cap de Nao there is a little road winding through the pines, and it is here that you will find the Hotel Bahia Vista, which enjoys a lovely view over the Bay of Jàvea. Six rooms are placed right in front of the swimming pool, and like those on the upper floor, they all have a private terrace. Our preference is for those on the brighter second floor, with number 3, under the roof, particularly attractive. Peter Dickens, an Englishman, is the manager and he takes great care of his hotel and insists that a very quiet atmosphere reigns. He is also very proud of owning a genuine English bowling green on the lawn, a rather curious game and a mixture between 'pétanque' and indoor bowling. Once the game-over, all repair to the bar to profit from the view, along with the restaurant. At only five minutes from the hotel, do not miss the superb walk near the Cap de Nao.

How to get there *(Map 22): 87km north of Alicante on the coast, and 7.5km from Jàvea on the road from Cabo de Nao.*

El Elefante ★★

03730 Jàvea (Alicante)
Carretera de 3 Cabanes, 19
Tel. (9)6-646 00 09 – Fax (9)6-579 50 08 – Sr y Sra Frith

Rooms 5 with bath. **Price** Double 6,000Pts, suite 8,000Pts. **Meals** Breakfast included, served 8:30-11:30. **Restaurant** Service 19:30-23:00; menu 1,900Pts, also à la carte. Specialties: regional and international cooking. **Credit cards** Visa, Eurocard, MasterCard. **Pets** Dogs not allowed. **Facilities** Parking. **Nearby** Cabo de San Antonio - Cabo de la Nao - Costa de Azahar to Valencia - Tosalet golf course (9-Hole). **Open** All year.

After spending fifteen years in the Middle East, John and Nadia Frith bought this house, which had the privilege of receiving Alfonso XIII when it was the only lodging house in the region. But why the Elephant ? Because in front of it there is a small mountain that looks strangely like such animal, and also because the owner has for a long time collected elephant-like objects, now scattered around the house. The greatest activity comes from the restaurant, while on the second floor five pleasant rooms, including that of the King with its private terrace, await you with their reasonable prices. Sun-tanning fanatics will delight in the large terrace-solarium on the roof, and will then refresh themselves in the swimming pool just close by which is surrounded by lawns. The cosy restaurant and bar have witnessed many an evening that finished far too late, for this place is much appreciated. This is a hotel without pretention but with a very warm welcome.

How to get there *(Map 22): 87km north of Alicante on the coast; before Jàvea, turn right, then Benitachell and the first on the left towards Cabo de la Nao.*

Huerto del Cura ★★★★

03203 Elche (Alicante)
Porta de la Morera, 14
Tel. (9)6-545 80 40 – Fax (9)6-542 19 10 – Sr Orts

Rooms 70 with air-conditioning, telephone, bath, WC, cable TV and minibar.
Price Single 13,500Pts, double 17,000Pts, suite 40,000Pts. **Meals** Breakfast
1,600Pts, served 7:00-11:00, full board + 7,000Pts (per pers., 2 days min.).
Restaurant Service 13:00-16:00, 20:30-23:00; carte. Specialties: Fish. **Credit
cards** All major. **Pets** Dogs not allowed. **Facilities** Swimming pool, tennis
(1,000Pts), sauna (1,000Pts), parking. **Nearby** The palm forest of Elche -
Church of Santiago in Novelda - Alicante. **Open** All year.

In the heart of Elche, a town known for its Paleolithic site and
its celebrated 'Lady', the Huerto del Cura ('curé's garden')
hotel will prove an agreeable staging post on the road to southern
Spain. The garden is a real oasis, particularly luxuriant, and
constitutes the main attraction of this parador built in the
'pavilion' style. The contemporary decor is without excess and
the many services are appropriate to this type of establishment; all
serve to create a relaxed atmosphere. The bedrooms are all quiet
and well-equiped, and decorated with contemporary furniture,
simple and in good taste. One may however regret certain details
of the decor (hanging ceiling lights), that rather annoyingly recall
collective institutes. Nevertheless, you will be sure to opt for a
bungalow, but somewhat away from the swimming pool for
greater quiet. The restaurant offers a rather jaded cuisine, said to
be 'international', but this is compensated by the pleasure of
lunching in the shade of the giant palm trees.

How to get there (Map 21): 19km southwest of Alicante.

V A L E N C I A

Hotel Montiboli ★★★★

03570 Villajoyosa (Alicante)
Tel. (9)6-589 02 50 – Fax (9)6-589 38 57
Sr José Manuel Castillo

Rooms 53 with air-conditioning, telephone, bath, WC, cable TV and minibar; elevator. **Price** Single 9,500-13,900Pts, double 15,600-23,500Pts, suite 19,900-31,800Pts. **Meals** Breakfast included, served 8:00-11:00, half board + 3,650Pts, full board + 6,200Pts (per pers., 3 days min.). **Restaurant** Service 13:00-15:30, 20:30-23:00; menu 3,650Pts, carte. Specialties: Fish and regional cooking. **Credit cards** All major. **Pets** Dogs allowed in the rooms. **Facilities** 2 Swimming pools, tennis, fitness club, sauna (1,000Pts), parking. **Nearby** Alicante - Guadalest - Don Cayu de Setea golf course (9-Hole). **Open** All year.

Facing full on to the sea, the Montiboli is a hotel 'de luxe' on a promontory and enjoying a very lovely site. A pretty path in the stone itself leads down to a first panoramic swimming pool, and on to a second on the level of the semi-private beach itself. Near to this one, a small restaurant serves paellas and seafood at lunchtime. Spacious, very bright and with pretty bathrooms, the rooms all have terraces. Most attractive are the bungalows with private staircase, lounge and open fireplace facing the sea. In the main building a very 'cosy' lounge with its beams visible and very light colored furniture, is next door to a reading room. The reasonable number of rooms allows for an attentive welcome on the part of the hotel, and you will be very much at ease here. You will certainly appreciate the lifestyle as you wake up looking at the sea, then lunch on the beach, and go to sleep in peace having dined under the stars.

How to get there *(Map 22): 32km north of Alicante via A7, exit Villajoyosa.*

193

R E S T A U R A N T S

A N D A L U S I A

ARCOS DE LA FRONTERA

El Convento, Marqués de Torre-soto 7, Tel. (956) 70 32 22. Pts 6,000.

CÕRDOBA

El Caballo Rojo, Cardenal Her-rero 28, Tel. (957) 47 53 75 - Elegant and refined, traditional cuisine with specialties such as *rabo de toro* (bull's tail) and *salmorejo*. - **Almudaina**, Campo Santo de los Mártires, Tel. (957) 47 43 42 - Closed Sundays. Close to the Juderia and the Alcazar gardens. Pts 4,000. - **El Churrasco**, Romeno 16, Tel. (957) 29 08 19 - Closed Sunday evenings and Mondays in winter. Touristy with flamenco in the basement, a pleasant ambiance however. - **Mesón El Burladero,** Calleja la Hoguera 5, Tel. (957) 47 27 19 - A simple *Taverne* with a very correct *Manolete* menu. Some tables in the patio in summer.

BODEGAS AND MESONES NEAR THE PLAZA TENDILLAS

Bodegas Campos, near the Plaza del Potro. - **Casa Rubio**, Puerta de Almodóvar 5. - **Mesón**

de la Luna, Calleja de la Luna.

CADIZ

El Faro, San Felix 15, Tel. (956) 21 10 68 - Welcoming decor, fish and seafood, Pts 3,800. - **El Anteojo**, Alameda Apodaca 22, Tel. (956) 22 13 20 - Another good fish restaurant.

GRANADA

Carmen de San Miguel, pl. de Torres Bermejas 3, Tel. (958) 22 67 23 - Closed Sunday, 15-30 August. In Alhambra, beautiful view on Grenade. – **Cunini**, Pescaderia 9 and Capuchinas 4, Tel. (958) 25 07 77 - Closed Mondays. The best fish restaurant in town. At the bar, a large variety of seafood tapas, Pts 3,500. - **Mesòn Andalus,** Elvira 17, Tel. (958) 25 86 61. - **Sevilla**, Oficios 12, Tel. (958) 22 12 23 - Correct cuisine, big tapas bar. Reservation needed. – **Ruta del Veleta**, road to Sierra Nevada (5km from Cenes de la Vega), Tel. (958) 48 61 34 - Closed Sunday evenings - Very good cuisine, grilled meat specialties, *carnes à la brasa*, and salted fish, Pts 4,000. – **Zoraya,** Panaderos 32, Tel. (958) 29 35 03. Beautifull terrace in Albaicin.

JAÉN

Los Maricos, Nuerva 2, Tel. (953) 25 32 06 - Delicious shellfish. - **Mesón Vicente**, Arco del Consuelo 1, Tel. (953) 26 28 16 - Closed Sundays. Regional cuisine, tapas bar and friendly dining room.

JEREZ DE LA FRONTERA

Gaitán, Gaitán 3, Tel. (956) 34 58 59 - Closed Sunday evenings. Andalusian cuisine and some Basque specialties, Pts 3,000. - **Venta Antonio**, road to Sanlúcar, km 5, Tel. (956) 14 05 35 - Closed Mondays. Banal and functional decor but good and well-cooked fish specialties. - **Tendido 6**, Circo 10, Tel. (956) 34 48 35 - Closed Sunday evenings. Beautiful andalous patio. Pts 3500.

TABASCOS AND MESONES IN THE SAN MARCOS QUARTER

Maypa, near the Plaza des Angustias - The best known. - **Venenzia-Faustino**, near the Place de l'Arenale.

MÁLAGA

Café de Paris, Paseo Maritimo, Tel. (95) 222 50 43 - Closed Sunday evening in winter. Pts 3500/5000. – **Antonio Martín**, Paseo Maritimo 4, Tel. (952) 22 21 13 - Closed Sunday evenings. One of the oldest restaurants of Málaga. Fish, paella, on a beautiful terrace over the sea. - **La**

Taberna del Pintor, Maestranza 6, Tel. (95) 221 53 15 - Specialties: Meats - Pts 3000/4000. - **El Boquerón de la Plata**, Alarcón Luyán 6 - the best bar for tapas and *gambas*.

FLAMENCO

Teatro Cervantes, a breeding ground of flamenco.

MARBELLA

La Fonda, Plaza del Santo Cristo 9, Tel. (95) 277 25 12 - On one of the prettiest squares in town, in an 18th century house, one dines on a marvellous patio. Very chic, Pts 6,000. - **Mesón del Pasaje**, Pasaje 5, Tel. (95) 277 12 61 - Closed at midday in summer. Victorian decor in the small dining rooms, international cuisine. Attractive and not very expensive. - **La Tricycleta**, Buitrago 14, Tel. (95) 277 78 00 - Closed Sundays and from January 15 to February 15. One of the best known restaurants in Marbella. Specialty, *Tricycleta brochettes*. - **Casa Eladio**, Plaza Naranjos 6 - Small and pretty ceramics-decorated patio.

TAPAS BARS

Bar Ana Maria, Plaza Santo Cristo - Closed Mondays. If not afraid of noise and a crowd.

MIJAS

El Padrasto, Paseo del Compás, Tel. (95) 248 50 00 - Beautiful view of Fuengirola and the coast. Classic Spanish cuisine. Pts 3,500.

NERJA

Pepe Rico, Almirante Ferandis 28, Tel. (95) 252 02 47 – Very pleasant in summer – Pts 2500/3000. – **De Miguel**, Pintada 2, Tel. (95) 252 29 96. Open the night October to March.

FLAMENCO

El Colono, Granada 6 – Flamenco in a typical Andalusian house. One can also dine here.

RONDA

Don Miguel, Pl. de España 4, Tel. (95) 287 10 90 – Closed Sundays from June to September. The restaurant is rather expensive but an attractive bar for having a glass and tapas, Pts 2,500. – **Pedro Romero**, Virgen de la Paz 18, Tel. (95) 287 11 10 – 'Bullfighter chic' ambiance, specialty *tocino del cielo al coco*, Pts 3,000. – **Mesón Santiago**, Marina 3 – Pleasant *taverne* in Andalusian style.

SANLUCAR DE BARRAMEDA

Mirador Donana, Bajo de Guia, Tel. (956) 36 42 05. Fish and seafood. Pts 3,000. – **Bigote**, Tel. (956) 36 29 96 – Fish, on the Bajo de Guia beach.

SEVILLE

El Burladero, Canalejas, Tel. (95) 422 29 00 – Closed in August. The favorite restaurant of the bullfighters, Pts 3,500. – **La Albahaca**, Plaza Santa Cruz 12, Tel. (95) 422 07 14. Closed Sundays. Beautiful Andalusian house of the famous architect Juan Talavera. Spanish and French cuisine, Pts 4,500. – **Egaña Oriza**, San Fernando 41, Tel. (95) 422 72 11 – Closed Saturday middays, Sundays and in August. Well situated above the Murillo gardens, a new restaurant appreciated by the Sevillians. Modern decor, gastronomic cuisine, Pts 5,000.

Hosteria del Laurel, Plaza Venerables 5, Tel. (95) 422 02 95 – Very touristic but well situated in the Barrio Santa Cruz. One dines on a terrace on the square, pretty house. – **Taberna del Alabardero,** Zaragosa 20, Tel. (95) 456 06 37 – In a old Palais- Pts 4000/7000. By reservation. – **La Dehesa,** Luis Morales 2, Tel. (95) 457 94 00 – Specialties: Meals. – **Rio Grande**, Betis, Tel. (95) 44 27 39 56. **Enrique Becerra**, Gamazo 2, Tel. (95) 421 30 49 – Closed Sundays. Only a few tables. Very lively tapas bar, Pts 3,500. - **Rincòn de Casana**, Santo Domingo de la Calzada 13, Tel. (95) 453 17 10 - Closed Sunday in July, ` August, Pts 3500/4500. – **El Mero**, Betis 1, Tel. (95) 433 42 52 - Closed Tuesday. Shell fish, Pts 3500.

TAPAS BARS

Alhucema, Carlo Canal 20 A. - **Cerveceriá Giralda**, Mateos Gago 1. - **La Estella**, corner of Calles Estrella and Pajarito. Savory tapas and not expensive. - **El Jovem Costalero**, Torneo 18. – **Casa Román**, Plaza de los Venerables. - **Cas Robles**, Alvarez Quintero 50.

Casa Morales, García de Vinuesa 11 - Unchanged since 1850, ideal for taking a *fino* (sherry). - **La Taquilla**, ideal for the bullfight days, facing the arena. - **Rincón San Eloy**, San Eloy 24. - **El Rinconcillo**, Calle Gerona 40 - The oldest bar in Seville (1670), tapas

and *tortillas de bacalaó*. - **Tremendo**, just next door, Calle San Felipe - Good beer accompanied by codfish and dried *mohama* (tunnyfish). - **Carboneria**, Plaza de las Marcedarias - Rustic, pleasant patio. - **Bar Garlochi**, corner of Calles Boteros and Alhondiga - Kitsch *'Semana Santa'* decor. Visit in the evening.

MORE CHIC: **Abades**, Calle Abades, for cocktails. - **Bar of Hotel Alfonso XIII**, for tea.

FLAMENCO

El Arenal, Dos de Mayo 26, Tel. (95) 421 30 75. - **Los Gallos**, Plaza Santa Cruza 11, Tel. (95) 421 69 81 - One of the best known spots, in the heart of the Barrio Santa Cruz. - **El Patio Sevillano**, Paeso de Colón, Tel. (95) 421 41 20 - Very, and too touristy.

A S T U R I A S
C A N T A B R I A

GIJON

Casa Victor, Carmen 11, Tel. (98) 534 83 10 - Closed Sunday evenings, Thursdays and in November. 'Nouvelle cuisine' fish restaurant. Friendly welcome.

OVIEDO

Casa Fermin, San Francisco 8, Tel. (98) 521 64 52 - Closed Sunday evenings. Sophisticated decor. Refined traditional cuisine, Pts 4,000. - **El Raitàn**, Plaza Trascorrales 6, Tel. (985) 21 42 18 - Closed Sundays in summer. Ideal for sampling regional specialties. No menu but 9 dishes regularly served, Pts 3,500. - **Del Arco**, Pl. de America, Tel. (98) 525 55 22 - Closed Sunday and August, Pts 3500/5000. – **Cabo Peñas,** Meaquiades Alvarez 24, Tel. (98) 522 03 20 - Typical restaurant, Pts 2500/3500.

BILBAO

El Asador de Aranda, Egaña 27, Tel. (94) 443 06 64 - Closed Sunday evenings, July 25 to August 14. Pts 3,500. - **Goizeko Kabi**, Particular de Estraunza 4, Tel. (94) 441 50 04 - Closed Sundays from July 25 to August 14. The grand, good and elegant fsih restaurant of the town. Pts 6,000.

B A L E A R I C I S L A N D S

MALLORCA
PALMA DE MALLORCA

Honoris, Camino Viejo de Bunyola 76, Tel. (971) 29 00 07 - Closed Saturday midday and Sundays. Pts 3,950. - **Porto Pi**, Joan Miró 182, Tel. (971) 40 00 87. Closed Saturday middays and Sundays. Old Mallorcan house. Basque 'nouvelle cuisine'. Pts 4,000. - **Bar Celler S'Antiquari**, Plaza Santa Cataline Tomás - Local clientele.

DEYA

Ca'n Quet, Carret. de Valldemosa, km 1.2, Tel. (971) 63 91 96 - Closed from October to April, and Mondays. Pretty view of the mountains. Pts 4,000.

IBIZA
IBIZA

S'Oficina, Avenuda de España 6, Tel. (971) 30 00 16 - Closed Sundays. The entrance is not very elegant but pleasant interior with patio. Basque cuisine. Pts 4,000. - **Bar San Juan**, Calle Montgri 8, Tel. (971) 31 07 66 - Bistro style. Good fish. - **La Masia d'En Sord**, Carret. de San Miguel, km 6.5, Apartado 897, Tel. (971) 31 02 28 - Open from Easter till October. Old house, art gallery. Pts 4,000.

SANTA EULALIA

Cás Pages, Carret. de San Carlos, km 10, (Pont de S'Argentara) - Closed Tuesdays and in February. Savory cuisine in this rustic old farmhouse.

SAN JOSÉ

Cana Joana, road Ibiza-San José, km 10, Tel. (971) 80 01 58 - Closed Sunday evenings, Mondays except in summer, from October 15 to December 29. Very pleasant setting in this old country house. Try the *riscalos* (mushrooms) and the *escallopinos de pato* (minced duck). Reservation advisable. Pts 4,000/6,000.

CASTILLA - LEON

AVILA

El Molino de la Losa, Bajada de la Losa 12, Tel. (920) 21 11 01 - Closed on Mondays in winter. Former 15th century mill in the middle of the River Adaja. Service in the garden on fine days. - **Mesón del Rastro**, Plaza Rastro 1, Tel. (920) 21 12 18 - In the wing of a medieval palace. Specialties: *El barco*, lamb and beans.

BURGOS

Mesón del Cid, Plaza Santa Maria 8, Tel. (947) 20 59 71 - Closed Sunday evenings. Well situated in a 15th century house. From the dining room on the upper floors, superb view of the cathedral. Good traditional cuisine. Pts 3,500.

LÉON

Casa Pozo, Plaza San Marcelo 15, Tel. (987) 22 30 39 - Closed Sunday evenings, from July 1 to 15. Simple and welcoming atmosphere under the attentive eye of Pin, the patron, who keeps his house well run. Pts 3,500/4,000. - **Adonias**, Santa Nonia 16, Tel. (987) 20 67 68 - Closed Sundays, 15 days in August. Regional cuisine in a rustic and lively setting. Pts 3,000/5,000.

BAR

Prada a Tope Bar, on corner of the Plaza San Martin - Tasting of regional wine from Bierzo.

SALAMANCA

Río de la Plata, Pl. del Peso 1, Tel. (923) 21 90 05 - Closed Mondays and in July. Small attractive restaurant serving a simple and quality cuisine. Pts 3,500. - **Chapeau**, Gran Via 20, Tel. (923) 27 18 33 - Closed August 15-31. Pts 3,500.

BAR

Café Las Torres, Plaza Mayor 26 - One of the best known bars on the square.

SEGOVIA

Mesón de Cándido, Mesón de Cándido, Tel. (921) 42 59 11 - Closed in November. All the personalities come here. An institution in Spain. Pts 3,000/4,000. - **Mesón de José Maria**, Cronista Lecea 11, Tel. (921) 43 44 84 - Closed in November. Equal with, and some say better than, its historical competitor. Pts 3,000/4,000. - **Mesón Duque**, Cervantes 12, Tel. (921) 43 05 37 - Intimate decoration and atmosphere for this other good restaurant of the town.

BAR

La Concepción, Plaza Mayor 15, close to the cathedral - The ideal halt for lunch.

SORIA

Mesón Castellano, Plaza Mayor 2, Tel. (975) 21 30 45 - Closed January 15 to 31 - Traditional restaurant. Specialties: *Chuletón de ternera, migas*. Pts 2,500/4,500.

VALLADOLID

Mesón la Fragua, Paseo Zorrilla 10, Tel. (983) 33 87 85 - Closed Sunday evenings, Mondays, in August. Luxurious, very expensive, frequented by the royal family. One of the best known restaurants of Castille. Pts 3,500/5,000.

CASTILLA - MANCHA

TOLEDO

Assador Adolfo, Granada 6 and Hombre de Palo 7, Tel. (925) 22 73 21 - Closed Sunday evenings. Major classic regional specialties such as *perdiz estofada toledana* and *delicias de màzapan.* Good wines selection. Pts 4,000/5,500. - **Venta de Aires,** Circo Romano 35, Tel. (925) 22 05 45 - On the outskirts of town - Good meats and generous Rioja wines. Pts 3,000/4,000.

BAR

In one of the small lanes south of the Plaza Zocodover, you will find numerous bars and small restaurants open on the sidewalks: these were used as decor in 'Tristana' by Luis Buñuel.

CUENCA

Figón de Pedro, Cervantes 15, Tel. (966) 22 45 11 - Closed Sunday evening, Mondays. One of the best known restaurants in Spain. Excellent regional cuisine. Pts 3,000. - **Mesòn Casa Colgadas,** Canònigos, Tel. (969) 22 35 09, Pts 4000.

PUERTO LAPICE

Venta del Quijote, El Molina 4. - Closed Thursdays and in September. Facing the church. Products of La Mancha in an ancient inn. Pleasant atmosphere, traditional and family cuisine. Pts 3,000/4,500.

G A L I C I A

LA CORUÑA

El Rápido, La Estrella 7, Tel. (948) 22 42 21 - Closed Sunday evenings except in summer and December 15 to 31. The shellfish are magnificent. Regular and elegant clientele. Reservation advised. – **Coral,** La Estrella 2, Tel. (981) 22 10 82 - Closed Sunday except in summer, Pts 2500/4500.

SANTIAGO DE COMPOSTELA

Anexo Vilas, Avenida Villagarcia 21, Tel. (981) 59 86 37. - Closed Mondays. Moncho Vilas is proud of having prepared the menu for Jean-Paul II's visit to St.-Jacques-de-Compastela in 1989. Good recipes from Galicia. Pts 4,000/5,500. - **San Clemente,** San Clemente 6, Tel. (981) 58 08 82 - Very good fish. Choose the more comfortable dining room. - **Bodega Abrigadoiro,** Carretera del Conde 5 - In the old town. Perfect for a lunch break (*chorizo* and *tortillas*).

PONTEVEDRA

Doña Antonia, Soportale de la Herreria 4, Tel. (986) 84 72 74 - Closed Sunday, Pts 3000/4000. – **Casa Solla,** Carretera de la Toja, 2 km, Tel. (986) 85 26 78 - Closed Thursdays and for Christmas.

C A T A L U N Y A

BARCELONA

In the town center.

Les Set Portes, Passage Isabel II 14, Tel. (93) 319 30 33 - The 7 doors in fact total 11 ! Paellas, rice in cuttlefish ink. Always lots of people. Pts 3,000/4,500. - **La Cuineta**, Paradis 4, Tel. (93) 315 01 11 - Typical restaurant in a bodega (17th-century).

3500/4500Pts - **Los Caracoles,** Escudillers 14, Tel. (93) 302 31 85 - Opened in 1835, success has never left it. Specialties: *Los Caracoles* (snails) of course, and *paella de mariscos*. The hot quarter in the evening. - **Can Ramonet**, Maquinista 17, Tel. (93) 319 30 64 - Closed August. Pts 3500/4500 – **Ca La Maria**, Tallers 76 bis, Tel. (93) 318 89 93. Closed Sunday evening, Monday, August. Pts 25000. – Agut d'Avignon, Trinitat 3, Tel. (93) 302 60 34 - Pts 4000/6000. – **Agut,** Gignas 16, Tel. (93) 315 17 09 - Closed Sunday evenings, Mondays and in July. In the Gothic quarter, an old house (since 1924) always offering well cooked Catalan specialties. Good wines selection. – **Egipte,** Jerusalem 12, Tel. (93) 317 74 80 - Behind the Boqueria market. Small restaurant on several floors serving regional cuisine at very affordable prices. 'Plat du jour' at midday

South

Ca l'Isidre, Les Flors 12, Tel. (93) 441 11 39 - Closed Sundays and July 15 to August 15. A classic of Barcelona, Catalan cuisine, chic ambiance. Go there by cab in the evening, the hot quarter. Pts 4,600/5,600. - **El Tragaluz**, 1 passage de la Concepciò 5, Tel. (93) 487 01 96 - Closed Sunday. Pts 5500. – **Els Pescadors**, plaza Prim 1, Tel (93) 309 20 18 - Closed Easter, Chrismas, New Year. Shell fish. Pts 3000/5000. – **Rias de Galicia**, Lleida 7, Tel. (93) 424 81 52 - Fish. Pts 4000/5000. – **Font del Gat,** passeig Santa madona Montjuic, Tel. (93) 424 02 24 - Closed Monday. Pts 4500. – **El Cellar de Casa Jordi**, Rita Bonnat 3, Tel. (93) 430 10 45 - Closed Sunday and August. Pts 2000/3000.

North

Botafumeiro, av. Gan de Gracia 8, Tel. (93) 218 42 30 - Closed in August. Specialties fish and sea food. Pts 4000/6500. – **El Asador de Aranda,** Avenida Tibidabo 31, Tel. (93) 417 01 15 - Closed Sunday evenings. Traditional atmosphere, decoration and cuisine. Pts 4,000. - **La Venta,** Plaza Doctor Andreu (at Tibidabo, served by the blue tramway) - Closed Sundays. Good fish and superb view of the city and sea. Pts 4,200/5,000. - **A la Menta**, passeig Manuel Girona 50, Tel. (93) 204 15 49 - Closed Saturday evening, Sunday in Juni to September. Pts 3000/4000.

Playa de San Miguel

Salmonete, Playa de San Miguel 34, Tel. (93) 319 50 32 - **L'Arrosejat,** Playa de San Miguel 38 - It is a Barcelona institution to go and eat paella and seafood on the Barceloneta beach.

'XAMPANYERIAS'

La Cava del Palau, Verdaguer i Callis 10 - Closed Sundays. Near to the Palau de la Música. Large choice of wines, champagnes and cocktails with sampling of patés and cheeses. - **El Xampanyet,** Montoada 22 - Closed Mondays. A lot of atmosphere in this 'xampanyeria', certainly one of the nicest in Barcelona, close to the Picasso Museum.

TAPAS BARS

Bar Rodrigo, L'Argeneria 67 - Closed Wednesday evenings and Thursdays. Near to Santa Maria de Canaletas church. One samples tapas with *vermut*, house specialty.

- **Cervecería Baviera,** Ramblas 127 - Sampling of tapas and seafood, at table or standing at the counter. - **Can Paixano**, Reina Christina, after the Plaça de Palau - Famous for its good 'cave' and tapas. Very modest prices.

CAFES

Café de l'Académie, Lledo 1 - Closed evenings. Near the Generalitat. Clientele of politicians taking a *bocadillo*. - **Cafeteria de l'Opera,** Rambla dels Caputxins - Beautiful café from the 'Belle Epoque' which has conserved its decor. Very good 'café au lait' (*cortado*). - **Els Quatre Gats,** Carrer. Montsio - Closed Sundays. Very famous café in a building (1896) of Josep Puig i Cadafalch, where Picasso had his first exhibition. Careful ! - a modern version is next to the old bar. - **Bar del Pí,** Plaça del Pí - Very popular 'Art-Deco' bar. Large outside terrace.

La Paloma, Carret. del Tigre 27 - Open Thurdays to Sundays from 9Pm. Vast rococo dance hall, surrounded by two tiers of seating where one finds all generations and social classes mixed together, rock and tango dancers. - **Bar**

Mundial, Plaça Santa Agusti Vell 11 - Closed Mondays. Very popular local bar for evening tapas. The back room serves *zarzuelas* and welcomes a more 'with it' clientele. Other specialty: peach liqueur (*melocotón*).

NEAR TO BARCELONA

MONTSERRAT

Montserrat, Plaça Apostols - Open only at lunchtime.

SITGES

Vivero, Paseo Balmins, Tel. (93) 894 21 49 - Seafood. Pts 2,300/4,500.

GERONA

Albereda, Albereda 7, Tel. (972) 22 60 02 - Closed Sundays. Pts 3,500/5,400. - **Isaac el Sec,** beside the museum - Tapas.

FIGUERAS

Ampurdán, Carretera de Olot, km 1.5, Tel. (972) 50 05 62 - Very good Franco-Catalan cuisine. Pts 4,500/6,000.

CADAQUÉS

Galiota, Narcis Monturiol 9, Tel. (972) 25 81 87 - One comes here for the fish and the Dali drawings on the walls.

TORTOSA

San Carlos, Rambla Felip Pedrell 19, Tel. (977) 44 10 48 -

The decor is without interest but do not be put off. The fish specialties such as *rosseyat*, fish from the Ebro delta, or *romasco de rape*, are excellent. – **Raco de Mig-Cami**, route Simpatica, 2.5 km, Tel. (977) 44 31 48 – Closed Sunday evenings, Mondays. Pts 2,550/3,500.

PUIGCERDÀ

La Vila, Alfons I. 134, Tel. (972) 14 05 04 – Closed Mondays. Very good cuisine. Pts 3,500. – **Madrigal**, Alfons I. 1, Tel. (972) 88 08 60 – Bar-restaurant serving tapas and some house specialties: snails, cuttlefish.

LLIVIA

(6km from Puigcerdá)
Can Ventura, Plaça Mayor, Tel. (972) 89 61 78 – Closed Sunday evenings, Tuesdays, in October. One of the good restaurants in the Puigcerdá area for its decor and cuisine. Reservation necessary.

MARTINET

(on the road 26km from Puigcerdá)
Can Boix, Tel. (973) 51 50 50 – Gastronomic restaurant with French and Catalan specialties. Good and expensive. Pts 5,000.

EXTREMADURA

CACERES

El Figón de Eustaquio, Plaza San Juan 12, Tel. (927) 24 81 94 –

Small restaurant very popular at lunchtime (reservation), well-prepared traditional cuisine, one of the best addresses in the region. Pts 2,500/3,300.

TRUJILLO

Hostal Pizarro, Plaza Mayor 13, Tel. (927) 32 02 55 – Convivial atmosphere in this small restaurant; Two sisters have taken over this family business. Keen to promote regional specialties such as stuffed chicken (*gallina truffada*).

NAVARRE

ARISCUN

Etxeverria, near to Frontón, Tel. (948) 58 70 13 – Pretty little inn in a former farm. Regional cuisine. Some pretty rooms.

PAMPLONA

Josexto, Principe de Viana 1, Tel. (948) 22 20 97 – Closed Sunday except in May and for the Saint-Fermin. Pts 6000/8000.

MADRID

MADRID

El Cenador del Prado, Prado 4, Tel. (91) 429 15 61 – Closed Saturday luncht, Sunday, 2 weeks in August. Pts 3000/4000. – **Posada de la Villa,** Cava baja 9, Tel. (91) 366 18 80 – Metro: Latina - Closed Sunday evening, 24 July to 24 August. In a old posada. Pts 6000/3000 – **El Mentidero de la Villa**, Santo Tomé 6, Tel. (91) 308 12 85 - Closed Saturday lunch, Sunday, August. Pts 4000/5000. – **Las Cuevas de Luis Candelas**, Cuchilleros 1, Tel. (91) 366 54 28. Pts 3500/5000. – **La Bola,** Bola 5, Tel. (91) 547 69 30 - Closed Saturday evenings, Sundays and in July and August. Cosy atmosphere. Traditional cuisine. Pts 3,000/4,200. – **La Dorada,** Orense 64, Tel. (91) 270 20 40 - Closed 3 weeks in August. The best for seafood and salted fish.

Café de Oriente, Plaza de Oriente 2, Tel. (91) 541 39 74 - Closed Saturday middays, Sundays and in August. Chic. In summer the most elegant terrace in Madrid to take a glass. One dines inside. Catalan cuisine. Basque cuisine on reservation. Pts 5,000. - **Botín,** Arco de Cuchilleros 17, Tel. (91) 266 42 17 - The Guiness Book of Records names it the oldest restaurant in the world, made famous by Hemingway. Specialties: *cochonillo* and *cordero asado.* Reservation necessary. Pts 3,000/5,000. - **Casa Lucio,** Cava Baya 35, Tel. (91) 365 32 52 - Closed in August. 'Taverne' freqented by artists, intellectuals, bullfighters. Traditional cuisine, very good Jabujo ham, reasonable prices. - **Casa Mingo,** Paeso de la Florida 2 - Closed Saturdays. In an old 'taverne' decor. Dinner outside in summer. Grilled chicken and Asturian cider. Ideal for lunch. Pts 800. - **Casa Paco,** Puerta Cerrada 11, Tel. (91) 266 31 66 - Closed Sundays and in August. Atmosphere of a real *'mesón'* (Catalan 'taverne'). Steakhouse specialties. Pts 2,000/4,000. - **Salvador,** Barbieri 12, Tel. (91) 521 45 24 - Closed Sundays and in August. Bullfighting restaurant decorated with photos and trophies. Family cuisine. - **Taberna Carmencita,** Libertad 16, Tel. (91) 531 66 12 - Metro: Chueca - Closed in August. Pts 4000. – **El Pescador,** José Ortega y Gasset 75, Tel. (91) 402 12 90 - Closed Sundays. Delicious fish specialties. Pts 5,000.

TAPAS BARS

Bocaíto, Libertad 6 - Reputed to serve the best tapas in Madrid. - **Las Bravas,** Alvarez Gato 6 - For its *papatas brava*s. - **Casa**

Alberto, Huerta 8 - Tapas eaten standing at the bar in beautiful wine cellar. - **La Chuleta,** Echegaray 20 - Bullfighting atmosphere. - **La Dolores,** Plaza de Jésus 4 - In a noisy ambiance, the best beer in Madrid accompanies the tapas. A few tables. - **Mesón Gallego,** León 4 - For its *caldo gallego*. - **The Reporter,** Fúcar 6 - For its trellised terrace. - **La Trucha,** Manuel Fernandez y Gonzales 3 - The tapas are delicious.

BARS

Café Gijon, Paeso de Recoletos 24 - One of the best known cafés of the capital. - **Chicote,** Gran Via 12 - Immortalized in Hemingway works. - **Los Gabrieles,** Echegara 17 - Little known by tourists. - **Hermanos Muniz,** Huerta 29 - Typically

Spanish. - **Cervecería Alemana,** Plaza Santa Ana 6 - Closed Tuesdays. Another Hemingway refuge. Tapas. - **Café Commercial,** Glorietta de Bilbao 10 - Superb, go and have a *café solo o cortado* (black or with milk). - **Bar Cock,** Calle Reina 16 (corner Alcala and Gran Via) -

Kitsch, to the glory of the famous Madrid barman, Don Chicote. - **Viva Madrid,** Calle Manuel González y Fernandez 7 - Old 'azuleros', tapas. - **Circulo's,** Alcala 42 - Magnificent 19th century café, base of the 'Cercle des Beaux-Arts' club. Frequented by artists and intellectuals.

FLAMENCO

EL Andalus, Capitan Hayas 19 - **Café de Chinitas,** Torija 7, Tel. (91) 248 51 35 - One of the best known and most touristy. Dinner served. - **Corral de la Pacheca,** Juan Ramon Jiménez 26, Tel. (91) 458 11 13 - Less touristy, more reasonable prices.

BASQUE COUNTRY

SAN SEBASTIÃN

Arzak, Alto de Miracruz 2, Tel. (943) 27 84 65 - Closed 3 weeks in June and 3 weeks in September. The reputation of the cuisine of Juan Mari Arzah has gone beyond the frontiers. Delicious Basque cuisine, delicious pastries. - **Salduba,** Pescaderia 6, Tel. (943) 42 56 27 - Closed Sundays and June 10 to July 10. Pts 3,000/4,000. - **Bodegon Alejandro,** Fermin Calbeton 22, Tel. (943) 42 11 58 - Closed Sunday evenings, Mondays, November 15-30, in February. Pts 2,800/4,600.

FUENTARRABIA

Ramón Roteta, Villa Ainara Irun, Tel. (943) 64 16 93 - Closed Thursdays and Sunday evenings except in summer. Very good cuisine served in summer in the garden of this beautiful old villa.– **Zeria,** San Pedro 23, Tel. (943) 64 27 80 - Closed Sunday evening, Thursday (except in summer), November. Pts 3500/4000. – **Kupela,** Zuloaga 4, Tel. (943) 64 40 25.

SANTANDER

Posada del Mar, Juan de la Cosa 3, Tel. (942) 21 56 56 - Closed Sunday, 10 September to 10 October. Pts 4000. – **Bodega del Riojano,** Rio de la Pila 5, Tel. (942) 21 67 50 - Closed Sunday evenings. Lots of charm and atmosphere in this former wine cellar. Seasonal and market cuisine. - **La Sardina,** Dr Fleming 3, Tel. (942) 27 10 35 - Closed Sunday evenings, Tuesdays except in summer. Pts 3,700/5,600.

V A L E N C I A

VALENCIA

La Hacienda, Navarro Reverter 12, Tel. (96) 373 18 59 - Closed Saturday middays, Sundays and in Holy Week. The chic restaurant of Valencia. Good classical cuisine. Reservation advised. Pts 4,500/5,800. - **Civera,** Lerida 11, Tel. (96) 347 59 17 - Closed Sun-

day evenings, Mondays and in August. Great specialist in grilled, poached and salted fish. Delicious but expensive. Reservation advised. Pts 4,500. - **El Timonel,** Felix Pizcueta 13, Tel. (96) 352 63 00 - Closed Mondays, Holy Week and in August. Very good fish cooked simply. Pts 3,500/5,000.

MORELLA

Mesón del Pastor, Cuesta Jovani 3, Tel. (964) 16 02 49 - Closed Wednesdays. Savory cuisine.

INDEX

S

T

INDEX